PRAYING ˈ
SUNDAY PS

C000023356

Richard Atherton

a redemptorist publication

(Year B)

Published by Redemptorist Publications
Alphonsus House Chawton Hants GU34 3HQ
www.shineonline.net

First printed November 2002

Design: Orchid Design

ISBN 0 85231 274 1

Printed in Britain

Redemptorist
PUBLICATIONS

Contents

Foreword

'But the Book of Psalms,' wrote John Paul II, 'remains the ideal source of Christian prayer and will continue to inspire the Church in the new millennium'. The Pope could hardly have expressed himself more clearly. The psalms, he tells us, are not simply traditional prayers, or helpful prayers, or powerful prayers, or even beautiful prayers; they are 'the ideal source of Christian prayer'. And he is confident that they will continue to inspire the Church in the new millennium, just as they have in the two millennia gone by – ever since those days when they were the daily prayer of Jesus himself.

The psalms hold a unique place in the Church's liturgy. They form the backbone of the Divine Office (or 'Prayer of the Church', as it is now known); they also feature in every Mass as responsorial psalms. In fact it is principally at Sunday Mass that the majority of the people of God first become familiar with the Psalter. Unfortunately, however, familiarity does not necessarily mean appreciation, and it is probably true to say that there is no part of the Mass less valued than the responsorial psalm. There are many reasons for this. Often the psalm is read badly, as though even the reader is not altogether convinced of its value; and even when that isn't the case, the congregation are usually so intent on remembering their line that they scarcely pay any attention to the psalm itself; and even when the psalm is read well and the congregation do their best to make it their own, there are still problems – in particular, many of the expressions, the ideas, the ways of thinking, even the theology of the psalmists can sound strange to a modern ear. Without in any way wishing to underestimate these difficulties, I believe that there is an underlying reason for them all – a failure to take the responsorial psalms seriously, to understand how they are connected with the other readings of the Mass, to appreciate their intrinsic value as prayers.

This book, like its predecessor, has been written in the conviction that, with a little effort and good will on the part of those who use them, the psalms will readily yield up their treasures. And so for each of the Sundays in 'Year B' a three-fold plan is provided. First, there is a brief commentary on the readings of that particular day, including an initial consideration of the responsorial psalm; its aim is to show how the whole Liturgy of the Word for that Sunday hangs together. Secondly, in the spirit of Mary, who pondered things over in her heart (Luke 2:19,51), there is a section headed 'Prayerful Ponderings'; its aim is to suggest how the responsorial psalm, when read through Christian eyes, offers much for our prayerful reflection. And finally there is a third section, which begins with the words 'Let us pray' – a reminder of the ultimate purpose of this book.

A little time spent with 'Praying the Sunday Psalms' will help those called to the ministry of reader to attune 'their minds …to their words', so that they understand what they are reading, appreciate its value and so are eager to communicate it as well as possible to their sisters and brothers. Judging from comments made about the earlier book in this series, preachers also may find these pages useful in preparing their homilies. Finally, and above all, it is hoped that all who read this book will find themselves better able to take that 'full, conscious and active part' in the Mass, so earnestly advocated by the Second Vatican Council; and might even find themselves moved to nourish their prayer during the succeeding week by returning to Sunday's psalm. One thing is clear: nothing will so help to ensure that the Psalter continues to inspire the Church during the third millennium of Christianity as the widespread praying of the Sunday psalms.

Once again, I wish to thank Rosemary Gallagher of Redemptorist Publications for her encouragement, and my brother Bernard for enriching this book with his attractive art-work.

[1] In his Apostlic Letter At the beginning of the new Millennium

[2] See The Constitution on the Sacred Liturgy §11

[3] *Ibid*/ 14

ADVENT

A shoot shall spring from the stock of Jesse

ADVENT

The Advent liturgy has a twofold focus:
it prepares us for the celebration of Christmas,
the first coming of Christ, and, in doing so,
directs our thoughts to his second
coming at the end of time.

First Sunday of Advent

Each of today's readings speaks in its own way of the (first or second) coming of Christ. The section from Isaiah (63:16-17; 64:1, 3-8) was composed at a time when the people of Israel, freshly returned from exile, were confronted with the apparently hopeless task of rebuilding their land. They call upon God, their 'Father', their 'Redeemer', to come to their help; they plead that he will 'tear the heavens open and come down'. That prayer was fully answered - in a way they could never have imagined - on the first Christmas Day.

The cry for God, the 'shepherd of Israel', to intervene on their behalf, is the theme of Psalm 79, from which today's responsorial psalm is taken. It's a cry not inappropriate for us as we prepare for Christmas.

In his first letter to his friends at Corinth (1:3-9), Paul assures them that the many gifts poured out upon them are a pledge of what is to come when 'our Lord Jesus Christ [is] revealed' at the end of time; and he expresses confidence that the Holy Spirit will keep them 'steady and without blame until the ... day of our Lord Jesus Christ'.

Jesus himself uses vivid imagery to warn his hearers that they must be ready for the day when he will come again: like a doorkeeper, they (and we) must be always alert, 'evening, midnight, cockcrow, dawn', so that his coming will not take us unawares (Mark 13:33-37).

Prayerful Ponderings

'God of hosts, bring us back; let your face shine on us and we shall be saved.'
Originally, this psalm was a plea for help in a time of national disaster; the fact that this refrain is repeated three times in the course of the psalm indicates the urgency of the plea. What precisely the situation was, we do not know. However, with a little imagination, the psalm can serve as a suitable prayer for the season of Advent, when, like those who awaited the coming of the Messiah, we long for his coming. Thus, we call upon him who bears the royal title of 'God of hosts' to 'bring us back'. The Hebrew word (*shub*) means, literally, 'make us turn' or 'turn us (and our lives) round': how appropriate, as we prepare for his coming, that we should ask the Lord to make us return to his faithful service. What makes the turning, and returning, possible is God's own loving kindness towards us; and so we plead: Lord, 'let your face shine on us' (with love and compassion) 'and we shall be saved'.

'O shepherd of Israel, hear us, shine forth from your cherubim throne. O Lord, rouse up your might, O Lord, come to our help.'
We go on to address him as our 'shepherd'/king; and beg him: first, to 'hear us' and our prayer; second, to 'shine forth' from his royal throne (the 'cherubim throne': the ark of the covenant was decorated with angel-like creatures which were thought to be at

the foot of God's invisible throne on earth); third, to 'rouse up your might' so that it may be felt; and finally, 'come to our help'. There's a kind of daring in the way the psalmist seems to tell God what he ought to do! But it's a daring based on the belief that we must never be afraid to speak frankly with God and at the same time on immense confidence in him and his readiness to hear our prayer. And so during Advent we might express our longing for Christ's coming by taking frequently on our lips the words of the first reading: 'tear the heavens and come down'.

'God of hosts, turn again, we implore, look down from heaven and see. Visit this vine and protect it, the vine your right hand has planted.'

The daring continues: this time God is urged to 'turn again' or even, as we might say, to repent. It seems as though God has deserted his people – hence the national disaster referred to above – and so he is asked to repent, to have a change of heart so that he will be ready to 'visit' and 'protect' his people once more. A vine was a prized possession, always tended with immense care. Here, as in other places in the Old Testament (e.g. Isaiah 5:1-7; Hosea 14:5-7), Israel is represented as God's own vine, 'the vine your right hand has planted'. There are times when we may feel that God has abandoned us or his Church; Advent is an appropriate occasion for us, following the example of our Jewish brothers and sisters, to plead that he will come once again and show his saving power in our midst.

'May your hand be on the man you have chosen, the man you have given your strength. And we shall never forsake you again: give us life that we may call upon your name.'

At first sight this verse seems to be concerned with an individual, the king for example. However, just as 'this vine' in the previous verse stood for Israel, so in this verse the expressions 'the man you have chosen' (literally, the man at your right hand, the place of honour) and 'the man you have given your strength' are other ways in which God's people identify themselves as God's possession. We Christians are his possession, too; and we also plead with him to come again, to make his saving presence felt. We share the confidence of Paul who declared: 'I am sure that he who began a good work in you will bring it to completion at the day of Jesus Christ' (Philippians 1:6); the saving work begun on the first Christmas Day will reach its completion when the Lord comes again at the end of time.

LET US PRAY: *Lord of hosts, during this season of Advent, may we foster a great desire for the coming of your Son; and, renewed in holiness, may we day by day be made ready for his coming again in glory - to judge and to reward.*

Second Sunday
of Advent

As we move another step forward in our Advent preparations, we hear a reading from 'Second Isaiah', composed by an anonymous prophet whose ministry coincided with the return of the exiles from Babylon (Isaiah 40:1-5, 9-11). It is a reading full of consolation and hope, together with the promise of one whose voice will be raised to 'prepare ... a way for the Lord'.

The gospel (Mark 1:1-8) reveals the identity of the herald. He is John the Baptist, who calls upon his hearers to prepare the way of the Lord, in particular by accepting a baptism which will be a token of their repentance.

St Peter (2 Peter 3:8-14) reminds us that with God a day is like a thousand years and a thousand years like a day. In other words, we are not to judge him by our standards: however long the world has to wait, he will come again, just as he promised; time is on his side.

The verses from Psalm 84 which make up the responsorial psalm reflect many of the ideas to be found in the first reading, as well as assuring us that God's promises will be kept.

Prayerful Ponderings

'Let us see, O Lord, your mercy and give us your saving help.'
This refrain, like other parts of Psalm 84, mirrors well the thoughts which fill our minds during the Advent season. We long to 'see' the Lord's 'mercy' (his covenant faithfulness), we long to receive his 'saving help'. The great feast of Christmas is the celebration of that 'mercy' and that 'saving help', made manifest in our midst in the person of a little child. The final and conclusive manifestation, however, will be when Christ comes again in his glory.

'I will hear what the Lord God has to say, a voice that speaks of peace, peace for his people. His help is near for those who fear him and his glory will dwell in our land.'
It looks as though in the original setting of this psalm a single voice, perhaps that of a temple priest or prophet, promised to listen for the answer to the prayer that had just been made; he is confident that when God speaks, what will be heard is 'a voice that speaks of peace ... for his people'. Now he announces the result: God's 'help is near' for all who reverently 'fear him' and 'his glory', his very presence, 'will dwell in our land'. In Advent we look forward with confidence to seeing God's glory dwelling with us in the narrow confines of a manger, set amid the straw of a stable.

'Mercy and faithfulness have met; justice and peace have embraced. Faithfulness shall spring from the earth and justice look down from heaven.'

The result of God's saving work on behalf of his people is now summarised by four of his characteristic attributes: 'mercy' (*hesed* or covenant loyalty), 'faithfulness' ('*emet* or steadfastness), 'justice' (*sedeq* or righteousness) and 'peace (*shalom* or general well-being). The psalmist depicts them – as perhaps only a poet could – now as meeting and embracing (to emphasise that they are working harmoniously for a common end), now as springing up 'from the earth' (or, perhaps better, from human hearts on earth), and now as looking down 'from heaven' (ready to appear as sheer gift of God).

'The Lord will make us prosper and our earth shall yield its fruit. Justice shall march before him and peace shall follow his steps.'

The Jewish people often saw temporal prosperity and a fruit-yielding earth as sure signs of God's favour, but we look forward to the Lord's coming, believing that it will bring the even greater blessings of spiritual prosperity and fruitfulness. The Hebrew version of the final sentence is unclear; it should perhaps read: 'Justice will march before him and make his footsteps a way'. Understood in this sense, it suggests that his 'justice', his concern with justice, good order, peace, is a way for us to follow. The Child of Bethlehem is someone not merely to be admired, or even to be loved, but to be followed.

LET US PRAY: *Knowing that Jesus is the 'only son of the Father, full of grace and truth', we pray that when he comes among us this Christmastide we may be ready to receive him with great love and faith.*

Third Sunday
of Advent

Amid the difficulties of rebuilding after the exile, the people hear a message from Isaiah the prophet (61:1-2, 10-11). Filled with the Spirit, he announces a 'jubilee year' when there will be freedom for all, when the land will be returned to its rightful owners and when Jerusalem will be restored and clothed in the bridal robe of justice and salvation.

Meanwhile, in the gospel (John 1:6-8, 19-28), John assures the people that though he is not the Messiah, but simply one who has come to prepare the way, nonetheless the long-awaited one, the one who will restore all things, is already present among them.

Paul (1 Thessalonians 5:16-24) insists that while awaiting the (second) coming of Christ, and with it the final and definitive restoration, people must be joyful, must pray, must give thanks and, above all, must do nothing to quench the work of the Spirit.

Mary herself, from whose Magnificat today's responsorial psalm is taken, can be seen as the perfect fulfilment of the description given by St Paul. She, like the prophet of the first reading, proclaims the faithfulness of God and the certainty of the restoration he will accomplish.

Prayerful Ponderings

'My soul glorifies the Lord, my spirit rejoices in God, my Saviour.'

Saluted by her cousin Elizabeth as 'blessed among women', as 'the mother of my Lord' and as blessed in her believing, Mary's immediate response is to raise her voice in praise of God. With 'soul' and 'spirit', with her whole self, from the depth of her being, she 'glorifies' and 'rejoices' in the God who is her 'Saviour'. As Christmas draws closer, and with it our salvation (our restoration to God's favour), we too ought to long to share in Mary's glorifying and rejoicing, perhaps especially on this Sunday which is traditionally know as 'Gaudete' ('Rejoice') Sunday.

'He looks on his servant in her nothingness; henceforth all ages will call me blessed.'

The fact that the Lord himself is shortly to come into our midst as a tiny child is itself an appeal to us to be humble and obedient. Mary is the embodiment of all that that means. It is because of 'her nothingness', her littleness, her humbleness of heart, that God 'looks' upon her with tenderness and compassion. As the Second Vatican Council expressed it, Mary 'stands out among the "poor" and "humble" of the Lord who confidently hope for and receive salvation from him' (Constitution on the Church, 55). She foresees that 'all ages will call me blessed', will continue what Elizabeth herself began when she hailed her as 'blessed among women'; but, with that honesty which is itself a reflection of genuine humility, Mary knows that her true greatness lies in the fact that she is the 'servant', the slave girl, of the Lord, totally at his disposal.

'The Almighty works marvels for me. Holy his name! His mercy is from age to age, on those who fear him.'
This prayer began with Mary magnifying the Lord, literally, making him great (by her praise); but he, 'the Almighty', has made her great, has worked 'marvels' for her, making her virginity blossom into Divine Motherhood. So it is 'his name', a Hebrew way of speaking of the reality of God, which is 'holy'. Like the Lord's Prayer, Mary's prayer calls for the hallowing of God's name. However, 'his mercy' – his compassion and love and graciousness – is for all time to come and for all 'who fear him'. In our coming Christmas celebrations we shall have the opportunity of learning once again of the generosity of our God.

'He fills the starving with good things, sends the rich away empty. He protects Israel, his servant, remembering his mercy.'
Throughout the Bible, and especially in the psalms, there is an emphasis on God's concern for justice, for the feeding of the hungry, for the protection of the weak. This divine concern, which has so often been re-echoed in recent statements by pope and bishops, is often represented, as here, in the black-and-white biblical terms of hungry people being fed and 'rich' people being reduced to penury. Advent is a time for us to examine our consciences about our attitude to the poor people in our world, for Christmas is not primarily about what we receive from others but

what we give to them – in view of what we have all received from the Lord himself.

The final assurance, that God 'protects Israel, his servant', seems to be a summary of all that has gone before; in the person of Mary, the person who is the embodiment of 'Israel', he has already shown his compassion. But it is with the birth of her Son that the era of salvation, of divine 'mercy', of restoration, will finally be inaugurated in the world.

LET US PRAY: *What more suitable prayer for this day than Mary's own Magnificat?*

Fourth Sunday
of Advent

God will not allow King David (2 Samuel 7:1-5, 8-12, 14-16) to build him a house (meaning, a temple); instead, God promises to build him a house (meaning, an eternal dynasty).

Though from the sixth century BC, when the people of Israel were taken into exile, there had been no king, yet God had not forgotten his promise. The angel that comes to announce to Mary her Divine Motherhood (Luke 1:26-38) tells her that her Son will be of the house of David – he is the Davidic king whose kingdom will have no end.

St Paul (Romans 16:25-27) recalls how the mystery of God's plan, kept secret for long ages, has now been revealed though Jesus Christ; and through him we come to understand how God's faithfulness is so much more wonderful than anything David and his successors ever imagined.

Psalm 88, or at any rate that part of it from which today's responsorial psalm comes, takes up the theme of the promise of a Davidic king, at the same time emphasising the love of God and his unfailing faithfulness.

Prayerful Ponderings

'I will sing for ever of your love, O Lord; through all ages my mouth will proclaim your truth.'
The first section of this verse is the refrain of the day's responsorial psalm. What more appropriate time to sing it than now as we prepare to celebrate God's 'truth', his utter faithfulness? When Jesus was born the promise made to David was fulfilled but in a way that exceeded all expectations. That is why Christmas, and the Advent season which leads to it, are times for singing of 'your love, O Lord', times for proclaiming the good news that God has been faithful, abundantly faithful, to his promises.

'Of this I am sure, that your love lasts for ever, that your truth is firmly established as the heavens.'
Even in the days before Christ's coming, the psalmists and their contemporaries were able to speak with confidence of God's love and faithfulness. With how much better reason we are able to do the same: we are 'sure' – there is the whole life and death of Jesus to substantiate it – that his 'love' is not simply a passing emotion but an attitude towards us which never changes, which 'lasts for ever'; similarly, we are confident that his faithfulness is as secure as the heavens above us.

'"I have made a covenant with my chosen one; I have sworn to David my servant: I will establish your dynasty for ever and set up your throne through all ages."'

At this point, God himself speaks, declaring that he has made 'a covenant', a bond of friendship, with David his 'chosen one'; more than that, he has 'sworn' an oath that he 'will establish [his] dynasty' and 'set up [his] throne' for ever. An interesting feature of this verse is that the word translated 'establish' really means 'build'. It takes us back to 2 Samuel 7 (today's first reading) and the pun on David's wanting to 'build' a house for God and God's promising to 'build' a living house for David. And that, in turn, turns our attention to today's gospel, where Mary is promised that 'The Lord God will give [her Son] the throne of his ancestor David' and 'he will rule ... for ever and his reign will have no end'.

'He will say to me: "You are my father, my God, the rock who saves me."'

As though in response to the previous verse, David is visualised as saying that he has discovered that God, 'my God', can best be described as 'my Father'; he has proved himself 'the rock' which brings me salvation. The repeated 'my' is an indication of the close bonds that link David with God. Through Jesus we have been given not only a clearer assurance that God is Father but also, in and through his own life, an indication of what that means. In similar fashion we are able to learn from the Child in the manger and the Man on the cross how wonderful the salvation that has been won for us.

'I will keep my love for him always; for him my covenant shall endure.

Again we can hear God himself speaking in this verse, giving David the assurance that he (God) will love him 'always', that his 'covenant' with him shall for ever 'endure'. But again, we also hear the Saviour who was born in Bethlehem assuring us of his love for us and the sureness of the new covenant which he has established in his life's blood.

LET US PRAY: *Lord our God, as we reflect on your unchanging love and your steadfast faithfulness, we beg that, despite all our shortcomings, we may make a return to you of abiding faithfulness and love.*

CHRISTMASTIDE

The Word became flesh Alleluia Alleluia

CHRISTMASTIDE

*This is the season in which we
celebrate the marvellous exchange
that has taken place:*

*We have been made sharers in
the divinity of Christ who humbled
himself to share our humanity.*

The Nativity of Our Lord, the Dawn Mass

In Scripture dawn is frequently represented as a special time, a time of grace, a time when favours can be expected from God, but also a time to turn to him again in prayer. Each dawn marks the beginning of a new day, but the dawn of Christmas day marks also the beginning of a new era for the human race.

In the first reading (Isaiah 62:11-12), the prophet looks forward to the city of Jerusalem being restored to the Lord's favour and recapturing her former glory. When that day comes the people will be called 'The Holy People' and 'The Lord's redeemed'. In fact through the incarnation of the Son of God we have indeed become the holy people of God, the Lord's redeemed; we're like a city that will never again be forsaken.

The second reading (Titus 3:4-7) declares that what has happened exceeds all expectations, for 'the kindness and love of God our saviour' have been revealed; more than that, through baptism we have become sharers in the salvation he has won and so can look forward confidently to 'inheriting eternal life'.

Meanwhile the gospel (Luke 2:15-20) records how the newborn Child received his first earthly visitors, the mountain shepherds, and how they, having seen and understood, went on their way 'glorifying and praising God'. As for Mary, she 'treasured all these things and pondered them in her heart'.

The responsorial psalm, which comes from Psalm 96, invites us to treasure and ponder the Christmas mystery, like Mary, and, with the shepherds, to glorify and praise God.

Prayerful Ponderings

'This day new light will shine upon the earth: the Lord is born for us'.
This response is a simple summary of the central theme of this morning's Mass: today a 'new light' shines, like a fresh dawn, upon all the earth because 'the Lord is born for us'; upon him our hearts ponder and to him we pour out our praise.

'The Lord is king, let earth rejoice, the many coastlands be glad'
This psalm, like the responsorial psalm at midnight, is one of the enthronement psalms, which celebrate the kingship of the Lord. However, when we use it today, the king we acknowledge and who brings joy to all the earth and to remote peoples in far-away lands, is none other than Mary's little son. Some six centuries before Christ was born earthly kingship had ceased to exist in Israel, but the people continued to declare that a king reigned over them and, as the following verses show, they wanted people everywhere to acknowledge him. Their king, they insisted, was God himself. Never could they have imagined that this almighty king would draw so close to them as today's gospel indicates, still less that he would be born of an unknown young woman from the nondescript little town of Nazareth.

'The skies proclaim his justice, all peoples see his glory'
The psalmist visualises people everywhere discerning the glory of the great king's presence and recognising his justice, that web of right relationships between God and humanity and within humanity itself, which his coming brings. The psalm pictures the very skies joining in the discovery; in a sense that is exactly what happened on Christmas day when the angel host gathered in the sky above Bethlehem and proclaimed the presence of the king and of his glory.

'Light shines forth for the just and joy for the upright of heart'
With the birth of Christ, a new and wonderful light has dawned for the human race, despite all the evil there may be in the world, and there is joy, joy beyond words to describe, for all men and women of good will.

'Rejoice, you just, in the Lord; give glory to his holy name'
A final exhortation that we may not merely reflect upon the joy our Saviour's birth brings but rather take an active part in the rejoicing and thereby 'give glory to his holy name'. Or, as the Jerusalem Bible expresses it, 'Rejoice in Yahweh, you who are upright, praise his unforgettable holiness'.

LET US PRAY: *Lord, we rejoice in the dawn of this glorious day. Give us a praising spirit like that of the shepherds who glorified God, a prayerful heart like that of Mary who treasured and pondered within her the wonders of this day.*

The Holy Family of Jesus, Mary and Joseph

Abraham (Genesis 15:1-6; 21:1-3) is called 'our father in faith'; it was faith that enabled him, then an old man with an aged wife, to believe God's promise that he would have innumerable descendants.

The letter to the Hebrews (11:8, 11-12, 17-19) also praises Abraham's strong faith (and Sarah's, too), especially when he was ready to meet the demand to surrender his only son.

In the gospel (Luke 2:22-40), Mary and Joseph express their faith both in presenting their child unconditionally to God as well as in the ordinariness of their daily life.

Today's responsorial psalm (104) gives thanks to God that he always has been, always will be, faithful to his covenant. In that sense, our faith in him is only a pale reflection of his faith in us.

Prayerful Ponderings

'He, the Lord, is our God. He remembers his covenant for ever.' In this refrain from today's psalm, we are reminded that 'our God' is a God who 'remembers'. It was not only in days gone by that he remembered; it is his nature to remember; he remembers still. He remembers, could never forget, the lifelong commitment which a couple make to each other, in his presence, on the day of their marriage. On that day he also gives them the assurance that he will always support them. 'Just as of old', says Vatican II, 'God encountered his people in a covenant of love and fidelity, so our Saviour ... now encounters Christian spouses through the sacrament of marriage. He abides with them ...' (Constitution on the Church in the Modern World, 48).

'Give thanks to the Lord, tell his name, make known his deeds among the peoples. O sing to him, sing his praise; tell all his wonderful works!' We are invited to 'give [him] thanks', to 'tell [forth] his name'; in particular on this day we are invited to thank him because the image most often used in the Bible to describe the covenant between himself and his people is taken from family life: namely, the close bond between husband and wife and that between parents and their children. In the measure that a family lives up to its high calling, it is making 'known his deeds' to all 'peoples'. Good family life is the outcome of a relationship between God himself and his creatures; the living out of such a life is the best possible way of singing 'his praise' and of telling forth 'his wonderful works'.

'Be proud of his holy name, let the hearts that seek the Lord rejoice. Consider the Lord and his strength; constantly seek his face.'

We are to be proud of 'his holy name', which is another way of saying that we are to be proud of our God. That in turn means that we are to trust him; married life is often very demanding – in the early Church it was sometimes described as a form of martyrdom; things haven't changed! – which is why it's so important that we 'consider' not simply our own small strength but 'his [mighty] strength' which he places at our disposal. For every couple, as for every individual, there is no substitute for 'constantly seeking his face' by daily prayer.

'Remember the wonders he has done, his miracles, the judgements he spoke. O children of Abraham, his servant, O sons of the Jacob he chose.'

It might seem a little odd to hear ourselves being addressed as 'children of Abraham' and the 'sons of Jacob', but, as St Paul reminds us, all 'those who believe are the descendants of Abraham' (Galatians 3:7). And so when we hear the exploits of 'Abraham', of his grandson 'Jacob' and of Jacob's own children, and of the 'wonders' and 'miracles' God did for them, we do so not as mere outside observers but as family. They are the stories of the beginning of a history which we inherit. Praise the Lord!

LET US PRAY: *Abraham your servant continued to believe even when all hope seemed to have vanished. Grant us, especially those of us whose high calling is in marriage and family life, a faith and a courage like his.*

Mary, Mother of God

In becoming man, Jesus took upon himself our humanity in its entirety. That meant that he was born in a particular time and place, that he became a member of a particular race, and the gospel recounts how, like any other Jewish male child, he was circumcised on the octave day of his birth (today is the final day of the Christmas Octave).

The first reading (Numbers 6:22-27) consists of an instruction on the blessing to be given by the priests. Was it a similar blessing that Jesus and Mary received when she took him to the Temple to be circumcised? The second reading (Galatians 4:4-7) teaches us that it is through Christ in his humanity, Christ 'born of a woman, born a subject of the Law', that God has given us the greatest of all blessings, a sharing in the divine life so that we are enabled to call upon him as 'Abba' (dear Father).

In the first part of the gospel (Luke 2:16-21), the shepherds visit the newborn Christ and worship him, and then go on their way blessing and praising God. The responsorial psalm is part of a thanksgiving prayer – Psalm 66; taking up the theme of the shepherds, it blesses and praises the Lord. Originally it was intended as a thanksgiving for the harvest, indeed it may have been composed for a harvest festival such as the Feast of Tabernacles. Only part of it is used in today's Mass; the explicit reference to harvest is absent, and that is unfortunate because today is the feast of Mary's motherhood, and Jesus, the fruit of her womb, is surely the richest harvest this world has ever witnessed.

Prayerful Ponderings

'God, be gracious and bless us and let your face shed its light upon us.'
These words are an adaptation of the blessing which, according to Numbers 6:24-26, Aaron and his sons were to use when they blessed the people. It is a blessing which the priests had pronounced over and over again throughout Israel's history. But never was the whole world blessed so magnificently as it was through the Divine Motherhood of Mary, for her Son is God's graciousness, God's blessing, the radiant smile of God's face made visible.

'So will your ways be known upon earth and all nations learn your saving help.'
However, it quickly becomes clear that the blessing of the Saviour's birth is to be spread over the whole earth. The good news of Bethlehem is to be taken to all the nations so that everyone will become aware of the wonderful ways of God and of his readiness to offer 'saving help' to all who are ready to receive it.

'Let the nations be glad and exult for you rule the world with justice.'
We Christians, like the Jews before us, find joy in the 'rule' and kingship of our God, and our prayer is that his 'justice', his impartiality and fairness, may be experienced by our brothers and sisters everywhere.

'With fairness you rule the peoples, you guide the nations on earth.' It was always Israel's prayer that their earthly king would function as shepherd of his people: his task was not simply to 'rule', but also to 'guide'; power and strength were to merge with tenderness and concern for those in his care. In Jesus we find just such a king; his is 'a kingdom of truth and life, a kingdom of holiness and grace, a kingdom of justice, love and peace'.

'Let all the peoples praise you, O God; let all the peoples praise you.' This psalm has links with two great Old Testament prophecies. The first is God's promise to Abraham that he will be blessed and then in his turn will be a blessing to all the families of the earth (Genesis 12:1-3). The second is the prophecy which emerges in Isaiah 40-55 that the salvation of Israel will be a revelation to all the nations that the Lord reigns and will lead them to praise him (for example 40:1-5; 45:21-25). In both cases Israel is the bridgehead by which God's blessing spreads throughout the world. It is through the Church, the 'sacrament' or effective sign of God's salvation, that the whole world is to be drawn to praise him.

'May God still give us his blessing till the ends of the earth revere him.' The responsorial psalm ends with this appeal that God will continue to favour us with such blessings that we in our turn may prove to be a blessing to 'the ends of the earth' – to everyone everywhere.

LET US PRAY: *Lord, we thank you for the harvest of blessings we have received from you, and above all for your dear Son Jesus, born of the Virgin Mary. We beg you to continue to bless us day by day so that we may bear witness to you unceasingly and others may thereby be drawn to you.*

Second Sunday after Christmas

Psalm 147 was composed for the congregation of Jerusalem which, after long years in exile, had returned home and set about restoring city and Temple. The people were filled with a desire to praise God for they knew that the reversal of fortune was due to God's intervention: that it was he who enabled them to rejoice once more in Jerusalem, to experience peace, to enjoy plentiful harvests; and that it was he who blessed them with his words and decrees.

At Christmastide – Christmas Day is still only a short time ago – we too are encouraged to raise our voices in praise as we recall all the good things that have come our way, thanks to the birth and life of Jesus. He has 'pitched his tent among us' (see the first reading [Ecclesiasticus 24:1-2, 8-12] and the gospel [John 1:1-18]); he has destroyed our alienation from God, raising us to dizzy heights as the adopted children of God (see the second reading [Ephesians 1:3-6, 15-18]); and he has drawn us into the 'Jerusalem' of his Church.

Prayerful Ponderings

'The Word was made flesh, and lived among us.'
These words are not of course part of the psalm – they come from St John's Gospel – but they are an admirable response to the psalm when it is viewed through Christian eyes. Our supreme reason for making this song of praise our own is that God has come to us in the person of Jesus Christ: he, the Word, Almighty Son of God, has taken upon himself our human condition and the consequences are wonderful beyond anything we could imagine.

'O praise the Lord, Jerusalem! Zion, praise your God!'
In the psalms the word 'Jerusalem' does not always refer to the city of that name; sometimes it means all the citizens, or even the whole people of God. And today we, God's people, pray this psalm to praise God for what he has done in building the 'new Jerusalem', his Church (which is itself a foretaste of the new Jerusalem of heaven), and for upholding it amidst all the eventualities of history.

'He has strengthened the bars of your gates, he has blessed the children within you.'
When the exiles returned, they had to look to the defence of their city; sturdy wooden bars ensured that when the city gates were closed they were secure. Within that security the people could again grow in numbers, after the terrible losses they had sustained.

Nonetheless, they saw within and above their activities the loving care of God for his people. As we pray this psalm we too thank God for the care he lavishes on his Church, ensuring that 'the gates of hell will not prevail against it' and blessing it in every age with new children in the sacrament of baptism.

'He established peace on your borders, he feeds you with finest wheat.'
This is another line which takes on richer meaning when applied to the Church, whose peace and essential unity God preserves despite scandals and setbacks and divisions. Above all, the Lord feeds us with 'finest wheat' – himself in the Holy Eucharist – and the first purpose of Holy Communion is to build up a common-union of love first with him and then with one another.

'He sends out his word to the earth and swiftly runs his command. He makes his word known to Jacob, to Israel his laws and decrees.'
The 'laws and decrees' given by God to his covenant people (Jacob/Israel) were seen as a revelation of his will and therefore as a precious gift. The distinguishing feature of this people was the fact that God had spoken to them, they had heard his word. And in the Church we rejoice in God's word, the Scriptures through which he reveals himself to us, and, above all, in his Word (with a capital letter) whose birthday we are now celebrating and whose teaching is our joy.

'He has not dealt thus with other nations; he has not taught them his decrees.'
Israel rejoiced in the singular gifts that God had bestowed upon

them. It was only with the passage of time that they began to realise that God's gifts, in particular his revelation, were not just for them but for the whole human race. There is no excuse for us Christians, however, if we do not recognise the universal implications of our Lord's coming. His last word to his disciples was that they should go forth and teach all nations, baptising all who would believe and bringing them into the bosom of the Church.

LET US PRAY: *We thank and praise you, Lord, for the gifts that you have bestowed upon us so generously. We ask you to keep your family in your peace and continue to sustain us with the bread of the Eucharist that we may be filled with a sense of security and of hope.*

The Epiphany of the Lord

The Epiphany is one of the oldest Christian feasts. It is not only older than Christmas, but also has a deeper significance, for rather than celebrating simply the birth of Christ, it also celebrates the whole purpose of his incarnation – the 'epiphany', that is, the appearance or manifestation of God through his Son Jesus. And so it serves as a fitting end to the Christmas season.

Today's first reading (Isaiah 60:1-6) is full of optimism: the people will be brought back home from exile and Jerusalem, once restored, will manifest the Lord to all peoples, drawing them from darkness into glorious light. Paul takes up a similar theme (Ephesians 3:2-3, 5-6): the secret at the heart of Christianity is that all peoples, Jews and non-Jews alike, are called to be members of the one Body of which Jesus is the Head.

Today's gospel (Matthew 2:1-12) also bears witness to the universal character of the 'good news', for it tells of the visit of the Magi, probably practitioners in the occult arts, who come from far-away lands with gifts – it seems that the practice of gift-giving at Christmastide arose from this episode – for the newborn King.

The responsorial psalm, taken from Psalm 71, with the response 'All nations shall fall prostrate before you, O Lord', chimes in well with the other readings: the Messiah King will be worshipped by all peoples, he will be reverenced and plied with gifts even by kings from distant lands.

Prayerful Ponderings

'O God, give your judgement to the king, to a king's son your justice, that he may judge your people in justice and your poor in right judgement.'
In all probability this psalm was composed for the coronation of a Davidic king in Jerusalem, but it is a portrait so utopian that no one could ever live up to its incredible ideals except that Messianic king who was born in the humble setting of a stable. He, as we know, is not merely the 'king's son', but the Son of the King of kings. That is why he can be relied upon to reflect 'your justice', a justice worthy of God himself, and to show a special concern for the poor, for they are God's poor ('your poor').

'In his days justice shall flourish and peace till the moon fails. He shall rule from sea to sea, from the Great River to earth's bounds.'
His reign, bringing with it 'justice' and every kind of well-being (*shalom*), will endure for ever – even 'till the moon fails', as the psalmist quaintly puts it. Just as the King's reign is endless, so his realm is boundless, 'from sea to sea', an expression which may refer to the promised boundaries of the holy land, from 'the Great River' of the Euphrates to the sea of the Mediterranean, or to the ancient notion that the earth was like an island in the midst of waters, so that 'from sea to sea' would be equivalent to from east to west.

'The kings of Tarshish and the sea coasts shall pay him tribute. The kings of Sheba and Seba shall bring him gifts. Before him all kings shall fall prostrate, all nations shall serve him.'

Whatever the precise location of 'Tarshish and the sea coasts' – the reference is perhaps to Spain – the expression is certainly meant to underline the fact that it is from the ends of the earth that kings come to acknowledge the King. There seems little doubt that in his account of the Magi's visit, Matthew had in mind the psalmist's reference to gift-bearing 'kings of Sheba and Seba'. A queen of Sheba once arrived in Jerusalem laden with gifts for King Solomon (1 Kings 10), but there is 'a greater than Solomon here', though born in a lowly stable.

'For he shall save the poor when they cry and the needy who are helpless. He will have pity on the weak and save the lives of the poor.'

Once more it is made clear that the long-awaited King will be full of compassion; he will have a special concern for 'the poor', 'the needy' and 'the weak'; indeed, he will have practical experience of the lot of the poor.

LET US PRAY: *On this day of Christmastide, we give thanks to you, Lord, for drawing us into the kingdom of your Son and enabling us to see in him the most perfect revelation of yourself. Like the Magi, may we bow low before him, offering the precious gifts of our faith, our hope and our love.*

The Baptism of the Lord

The feast of the Baptism of our Lord, on the Sunday after the Epiphany, always takes the place of the first Sunday in Ordinary Time. Today's first reading (Isaiah 55:1-11) is in the form of an invitation to a joyful banquet, an image frequently used in the Old Testament to indicate God's love for his people; here, the banquet is to celebrate a new covenant that God is to make and it is for the poor - those who hunger for God, those who thirst for his word.

The One who can satisfy that hunger and thirst is Jesus Christ (Mark 1:7-11), who as he emerges from the baptismal waters is acknowledged as 'my Son, the Beloved'. He is the new covenant in person. Like the rain and the snow (see first reading), he has come down from heaven and he will not return without doing his Father's will and achieving our salvation.

The second reading (1 John 5:1-9) declares that 'whoever believes that Jesus is the Christ' is a child of God; it is in that sharing in his divine sonship that our salvation consists.

Exceptionally, today's responsorial psalm (Isaiah 12:2-6) is one of the psalms from the Old Testament which does not appear in the Psalter, and is usually known, technically, as a canticle. It speaks in joyful tones of the salvation won for us, the new covenant forged for us, while at the same time calling upon us to make 'these marvellous deeds' known to others.

Prayerful Ponderings

'With joy you will draw water from the wells of salvation.'
This refrain serves as a bold announcement that Jesus is the new covenant, the fountain 'of salvation'. Therefore, all are joyfully invited to come and 'draw water' at this source, remembering, as the first reading told us, that it is all 'at no cost', it is freely given. Our task is only to receive, to open ourselves to God's gift offered us through Jesus.

'Truly God is my salvation, I trust, I shall not fear. For the Lord is my strength and my song, he became my saviour.'
As we visualise Jesus emerging from the waters of the Jordan, we might address him in the words of this verse: 'Truly' you are 'my salvation' and so 'I trust' you and 'shall not fear', whatever may befall me. After all, you are 'my strength' (the one on whom I depend), 'my song' (of joy and happiness) and 'my saviour' (why, your very name, Jesus [*Yeshua*], means Saviour).

'Give thanks to the Lord, give praise to his name! Make his mighty deeds known to the peoples! Declare the greatness of his name.'
In the thrill of recognising that Jesus has come as our Saviour, we delight to 'give thanks to the Lord', to 'give praise to his name', to do what we can to 'make his mighty deeds known to [all] the peoples',

to 'declare the greatness of his name'. But of course what matters is not simply what we decide – or even declare – at our Sunday Mass, but what we do about it on all the other days of the week.

'Sing a psalm to the Lord for he has done glorious deeds, make them known to all the earth! People of Zion, sing and shout for joy for great in your midst is the Holy One of Israel.' Again the call goes forth to praise God ('sing a psalm to the Lord') for the 'glorious deeds' he has done and proclaim them 'to all the earth'. 'Zion', or Jerusalem, drew its religious significance from the fact that God himself was believed to dwell there, first in the ark of the covenant and then in the Temple. That is why the people were called upon to 'sing and shout' for 'the Holy One' in their midst. We are the people of the new Zion, living stones making up a temple (see 1 Corinthians 3:16; Ephesians 2:21-22); and, above all when we gather as a redeemed and worshipping community, we too rejoice in the knowledge that in our very midst is 'the Holy One', our three-personed God.

LET US PRAY: *We rejoice, Lord God, and give thanks that Jesus Christ, your beloved Son, has forged a new covenant between you and us, and thereby won our salvation. May we, who have had the joy of being baptised, be strong and courageous in striving to live out the implications of our baptism in our daily lives.*

LENT

*By
his sufferings
shall
my servant
justify
many*

LENT

*Lent, the Church's season of
preparation for Easter, is marked
by two related themes: baptism
(already received or due to be received at Eastertime)
and penitence.*

First Sunday of Lent

On this the first Sunday of Lent, we are confronted with what the Second Vatican Council calls one of the 'elements ... especially characteristic of Lent' (Constitution on the Sacred Liturgy, 109), namely the sacramental covenant of baptism. In the first reading (Genesis 9:8-15) we hear how God made a covenant of peace with Noah and his family, a covenant symbolised by the rainbow.

Peter, in the second reading (1 Peter 3:18-22), reminds us that just as Noah's people were saved by the ark, so we are saved by baptism which is itself the means of our participation in the dying and rising of Jesus.

As we enter into this 'desert' period of Lent, we should find encouragement in the account of our Lord's temptations in the desert (Mark 1:12-15). Their successful outcome marks the beginning of the ultimate conquest of sin. Already Jesus can declare 'the kingdom of God is close at hand'.

The responsorial psalm, taken from the first verses of Psalm 24, is filled with hope, just as the other readings are, and asks that, as we begin Lent, we may follow 'his way'.

Prayerful Ponderings

'Your ways, Lord, are faithfulness and love for those who keep your covenant.'

Here in simple words is the reason why we strive to maintain the 'covenant' which he has made (or, if we are preparing for entry into the Church, is soon to make) with us. His 'ways' – his values, his ideals, his will – all reflect his covenant 'faithfulness and love'. They are all in our interest, and at the same time serve as an inspiration for us to maintain our part of the covenant relationship to the best of our ability.

'Lord, make me know your ways. Lord, teach me your paths. Make me walk in your truth, and teach me: for you are God my saviour.'

An earnest plea, most suitable for this season of Lent, that the 'Lord' may make known to me his 'ways', teach me his 'paths', make me 'walk in [his] truth'. But the biblical word 'know' doesn't simply mean 'know about' (in the way I might know about astrology or IT or mathematics); it suggests intimacy, knowledge from the inside (in the way that husband and wife know each other). What I am asking of God, is that I might know from the inside, as it were, all that I have ever learned about him, so that truths of faith may come alive for me. Wasn't that what Jesus implied when he spoke of himself as the Way, the Truth and the Life?

'Remember your mercy, Lord, and the love you have shown from of old. In your love remember me, because of your goodness, O Lord.'

'Remember' is a strong word in the Bible, one that often implies compassionate concern for what is remembered: as one scholar puts it, 'God's remembering always implies his movement towards the object of his memory' (Brevard Childs). So, I ask God in his 'love' to 'remember me', to move towards me with compassion; indeed, if there should be any doubt why I want him to remember, I ask explicitly that he will 'remember [his] mercy' in my regard and 'the love that [he has] shown from of old'. I ask with confidence and the grounds for my confidence are quite simply 'your goodness, O Lord'.

'The Lord is good and upright. He shows the path to those who stray, he guides the humble in the right path; he teaches his way to the poor.'

'The Lord is good and upright' in himself, and therefore with us. He expresses that goodness, that uprightness, in the way he 'shows' and 'guides' and 'teaches', in his gentle patience not only with 'the humble' and 'the poor', which is what we might expect, but also with 'those who stray'. During Lent especially we can never be reminded too often that Jesus, on his own admission, came 'not to call the just but sinners to repentance'; sinners – and that includes us – are his concern.

LET US PRAY: *As we begin the season of Lent, we pray that all that we do in the way of Lenten exercises will be directed towards growing in knowledge and love of our Lord Jesus Christ, and so of walking in his ways and consolidating that covenant of friendship which he established with us at baptism.*

Second Sunday
of Lent

The responsorial psalm, an excerpt from Psalm 115, expresses the gratitude and relief of someone who underwent terrible suffering and almost despaired of escaping alive, but was finally rescued by God.

It's the kind of prayer that Abraham might have said (Genesis 22:1-2, 9-13, 15-18) as he came down from Mount Moriah, his son Isaac by his side. Abraham in fearful anguish had obeyed God and God in his turn had intervened, ensuring that the promise to Abraham of an innumerable progeny would not be cancelled.

St Paul, however, speaks of the extraordinary paradox that the God who saved Isaac did not spare his own dear Son, but allowed him to be delivered up to death for our sakes (Romans 8:31-34). Here is the supreme proof of his love for us. Yet even that is not the end of the story, for his Son, now risen, 'pleads for us' with the Father.

The gospel (Mark 9:2-10) recalls the transfiguration when the disciples caught a glimpse of Jesus' hidden glory. With it came the assurance that though he was destined to die, he would rise from the dead.

Prayerful Ponderings

'I will walk in the presence of the Lord in the land of the living.'
This refrain is the psalmist's grateful response after being rescued by God from impending disaster; hence the resolve to be faithful to 'the Lord', walking 'in [his] presence' so long as life shall last. We may not have had an experience similar to that of the psalmist, and yet, as we have good reason to remember in this season of the year, we have been rescued from a peril far greater than the psalmist's - that of forfeiting heaven - until the Lord himself intervened through his Son Jesus. We too therefore should feel an obligation to strive to 'walk in the presence of the Lord' all our days.

'I trusted, even when I said: "I am sorely afflicted."'
These simple words express enormous trust. None of us has much difficulty in trusting in God, so long as all goes well. But when things seem to be going dreadfully badly, when God seems to have forgotten us or to be asking the impossible of us (only think of Abraham, called by God to sacrifice his only son), when we are 'sorely afflicted' - then is the time when the true nature of our trust is laid bare.

'O precious in the eyes of the Lord is the death of his faithful.'
In the original psalm, the word 'precious' is ambiguous. It might mean 'highly valued'; it might also mean 'costly'. If we think of the Lord's 'faithful' one par excellence, his Son, Jesus, then both senses are wonderfully apposite: his 'death' was highly valued by the

Father – so much so that it won our redemption; but to a Father who is aware of the fall of a tiny sparrow (Matthew 10:29) that 'death' also cost him dearly.

'Your servant, Lord, your servant am I; you have loosened my bonds. A thanksgiving sacrifice I make: I will call on the Lord's name.'

The psalmist, conscious of the way in which God has 'loosened my bonds' (whatever they may have been), now is glad to be called 'your servant', and is ready to offer 'a thanksgiving sacrifice' and 'call on the Lord's name' in prayer. Reflecting on all that the Lord has done for us – by loosening the 'bonds' of our sins on the cross – we should be more eager than the psalmist to number ourselves among God's servants, to invoke him in prayer and to offer the great 'thanksgiving sacrifice', the Eucharist.

'My vows to the Lord I will fulfil before all his people, in the courts of the house of the Lord, in your midst, O Jerusalem.'

The psalmist is so grateful that he wants his gratitude to be shown publicly, and so promises to 'fulfil' 'before all [the] people' the 'vows' that were made when danger threatened, and to do so in 'Jerusalem', in 'the house of the Lord'. One of the most important aspects of our weekly Mass is that it gives us the opportunity to express publicly, along with our brothers and sisters, our gratitude for all that 'the Lord' has done for us. All this takes on deeper significance when it is recalled that this psalm, composed for the use of an individual, eventually became part of the liturgy of a larger community and in fact took its place as one of a group of psalms that were always sung at the Passover. It is, therefore, a psalm which Jesus himself would have prayed in the course of the Last Supper.

LET US PRAY: *Keep us ever mindful, Lord, of all that you have accomplished for us through your Son, Jesus Christ. May the memory of your limitless love fill us always with gratitude and the desire to be for ever your faithful servants.*

Third Sunday of Lent

Having rescued his people from slavery, God gives them the Ten Commandments, a charter of freedom, if only they will remain faithful (Exodus 20:1-17).

The gospel (John 2:12-25) indicates that many of the people have not remained faithful, for in their greed they have turned the Temple, God's own dwelling-place, into a market-place. As Jesus ejects the buyers and sellers, he announces that the true temple, the place where God is indeed to be found, is to be himself, when he has risen from the dead.

Paul (1 Corinthians 1:22-25) reflects on Jesus' death, which, though interpreted by many as a sign of weakness or foolishness, is in fact a demonstration to the world of God's power and wisdom.

The responsorial psalm comes from Psalm 18, which hymns the wonders of God's law. Unusually, the refrain comes not from the psalm but from the Gospel of John: 'You, Lord, have the message of eternal life.' But it is, as we shall see, completely in harmony with the psalm, and enables us to express our wholehearted allegiance to that charter of God which consists not only of the Ten Commandments but of the whole of his revelation - summed up in his Son, Jesus.

Prayerful Ponderings

'The law of the Lord is perfect, it revives the soul.'

Each of the first six lines of this attractive poem consists of three elements: first, the word 'law', or a synonym for it - there are so many ways of describing it because it means more than simply the Ten Commandments – perhaps 'God's will' best sums it up; second, a single descriptive adjective; and third a brief comment on its effects. So, the first thing we learn about God's law is that it is 'perfect', flawless, unalloyed. As Paul will explain in his letter to the Romans, we are 'not to be conformed to this world' but rather to 'be transformed' by discerning 'what is the will of God - what is good and acceptable and perfect' (12:2). Its effect is that 'it revives the soul', it restores our innermost self as surely as food and sleep restore us physically.

'The rule of the Lord is to be trusted, it gives wisdom to the simple.'

God's revelation may be described as a 'rule' but it is a rule 'to be trusted': it is completely reliable, it will never let us down. It gives 'wisdom', even, perhaps especially, to those whom the world at large considers 'simple'. It is refreshing to meet an individual who by the world's standards is not very bright or gifted, and yet has a 'wisdom', an understanding and appreciation of life, that many of the highly educated and richly talented clearly lack.

'The precepts of the Lord are right, they gladden the heart.'
'Precepts' is yet another way of describing the instruction and guidance that God gives us. They are 'right' in the sense that they guide us in the right path, and at the same time they bring joy to 'the heart'; that is why the truly righteous person has a joy which nothing can take from him or her.

'The command of the Lord is clear, it gives light to the eyes.'
'The command of the Lord' – here we might think of what Jesus called 'the first' of all the commandments, as well as the second which, he said, is like to it: 'You shall love the Lord your God with all your heart, and with all your soul, and with all your mind, and with all your strength'; and 'You shall love your neighbour as yourself' (see Mark 12:29-31). There is a clarity, a directness, about this twofold command of love, which enlightens us in every area of life.

'The fear of the Lord is holy, abiding for ever.'
Reverential 'fear of the Lord', and of all that he has revealed, is already the beginning of holiness. It brings with it an awe, and a readiness to do God's will that are to be found at their best in those who are in heaven. That is why Eucharist Prayer II can refer to Our Lady and the saints simply as those 'who have done your will throughout the ages'.

'The decrees of the Lord are truth and all of them just.'
God's 'decrees', all that he has made known to us in revelation, possess 'truth', not simply in the sense that they are not false, but rather in the sense that they are to be depended upon as in our own best interests, and 'until heaven and earth pass away' his word will

not pass away (Matthew 5:18). All that the Lord has revealed is of a piece: it is 'just', righteous.

'They are more to be desired than gold, than the purest of gold and sweeter are they than honey, than honey from the comb.' After all that has been said, it is little wonder that the poet sums up by speaking of God's law as 'more to be desired than gold', even 'the purest of gold', and 'sweeter... than honey' from the honeycomb.

LET US PRAY: *On this day, Lord, when we ponder your love, clearly displayed in the sufferings and death of Christ, we ask that we may be convinced that your law also is a token of your love and therefore always for our good.*

Fourth Sunday of Lent

Today is traditionally known as 'Laetare (Rejoice!) Sunday' and the readings of the Mass suggest many reasons for rejoicing. The reading from Chronicles, after describing the destruction of Jerusalem and the days of exile, shows how God, through the Persian king, Cyrus, brought his people home (1 Chronicles 36:14-16, 19-23).

But of course we, the whole of humankind, have an infinitely more wonderful Saviour than Cyrus. Paul tells us (Ephesians 2:4-10) that God so loved us that, through his Son Jesus, he has brought us back to life from the exile/death of sin, and already, in Jesus, given us a way home to heaven itself.

The gospel (John 3:14-21) tells us that Christ 'lifted up' - on the cross and in his resurrection - brings salvation to all who believe in him. For he came into the world not to condemn but to save.

The responsorial psalm, Psalm 136, recalls the bitter days of exile in Babylon. After the exile was over, it served as a perpetual reminder of what God had done for them - and it serves us as a reminder of the still more wonderful salvation that he has accomplished through Jesus, by rescuing us from the exile brought upon us by our sins. We may find it a help towards making prayerful use of this psalm to realise that 'Babylon' can stand as a symbol for all that threatens human happiness - suffering, hatred, sin, wickedness.

Prayerful Ponderings

'By the rivers of Babylon there we sat and wept, remembering Zion; on the poplars that grew there we hung up our harps.'
Unlike other psalms, Psalm 136 is specific in its reference to time, place and event. It looks back to the time when 'Zion' was razed to the ground by the Babylonians, that is to say, towards the end of the sixth century BC. It recalls how the exiles 'sat and wept', as they remembered happier times, and how they 'hung up [their] harps' on the branches of 'the poplars that grew there', for they knew that this was no time for music-making. It also tells where this happened: besides the streams (probably the system of canals) that ran through the plain where 'Babylon' was sited.

'For it was there that they asked us, our captors, for songs, our oppressors, for joy. "Sing to us," they said, "one of Zion's songs."'
The returned exiles grimly recall how their 'captors' had taunted them to 'sing to us one of Zion's songs'. The reference may have been to songs about Jerusalem, but, more likely, it was to hymns in general in praise of Yahweh. To have sung such songs in enemy territory would have been more than acquiescing to the demands of 'oppressors', it would have been an act of disloyalty, tantamount to a denial of faith.

'O how could we sing the song of the Lord on alien soil? If I forget you, Jerusalem, let my right hand wither!'
It was simply unthinkable in these circumstances that they should

'sing the song of the Lord'. The very idea of such an act of betrayal leads the psalmist to address 'Jerusalem' directly in the form of an oath: better a withered 'right hand' than to use that hand, in forgetfulness of the holy city, to pluck the strings of the harp, as had been requested.

'O let my tongue cleave to my mouth if I remember you not, if I prize not Jerusalem above all my joys!'
The oath continues: better to be afflicted with dumbness (my tongue cleaving uselessly to 'my mouth') than failing to 'prize ... Jerusalem above all my joys', to use that tongue to sing songs of Zion for the enemy. The book of Revelation speaks of the two cities, Babylon and Jerusalem, the first 'the great prostitute'(Revelation 18), the second 'the new Jerusalem' (Revelation 21:2), our heavenly homeland. During our life on this earth, as St Augustine suggests, these two cities compete for our hearts. Today's psalm give us the opportunity to reaffirm that our hearts are resolutely set upon the heavenly Jerusalem.

LET US PRAY: *God our Father, as we live through our days of exile on earth, help us never to be so seduced by the attractions of this earthly Babylon that we fail to prize our heavenly Jerusalem above all other joys.*

Fifth Sunday of Lent

The first reading (Jeremiah 31:31-34) brings us the famous prophecy of Jeremiah that a time will come when God will create 'a new covenant' with his people, a covenant which will mean that his law, his instruction, will not be written on stone but rooted in the human heart.

The second reading (Hebrews 5:7-9) and the gospel (John 12:20-30) remind us that the creation of this new covenant will cost God dearly: it will involve his beloved Son, says the letter to the Hebrews, in 'entreaty', 'silent tears' and 'suffering'; it will mean, says the gospel, that Jesus will be like 'a grain of wheat' which must surely die and be buried if it is to bear fruit.

Finally, the responsorial psalm, drawn from the penitential Psalm 50, pleads for the creation of 'a pure heart' in us, a pure heart that will enable the Lord to fashion the new covenant with us.

Prayerful Ponderings

'Have mercy on me, God in your kindness. In your compassion blot out my offence.'

Today's psalm reminds us that one of the graces of Lent is a recognition of our sinfulness, and, therefore, of our need for the 'compassion' and limitless 'mercy' of God. We pray that in his loving 'kindness' he will 'blot out [our] offence'. The use of the singular – 'offence' rather than 'offences' – does not mean that we are aware of only one sin, but rather that all our sins contribute to a global state of sinfulness from which we long to be set free. Just as this psalm uses three words to describe sin, suggesting, respectively, that it involves a missing of the mark, rebellion and crookedness, so it uses three words to express the process of forgiveness. The first of them appears in this verse: to 'blot out', which is taken from a verb meaning to cancel or obliterate; we ask that our 'offence' may be erased, like an error in an exercise book.

'O wash me more and more from my guilt and cleanse me from my sin.'

The other two words appear in this verse. 'Wash me more and more from my guilt': wash away my sins thoroughly, in the way that soiled clothing is laundered by its being trampled underfoot. 'And cleanse me from my sin': wash me not merely by a superficial sprinkling of water but by making me morally clean deep within.

'A pure heart create for me, O God, put a steadfast spirit within me.'

If the cleansing process sounds unduly negative, then here is its positive aspect: we ask God not simply to take away our sins but, at the same time, to create in us 'a pure heart', a heart that is set on doing the Father's will, a heart that is ready for the closest covenant relationship with him. Moreover, our prayer is that we may be given 'a steadfast spirit within', to keep us faithful and unwavering when temptations abound. By 'spirit' the psalmist may have thought simply in terms of a strengthened will, but what we beg for is that the Spirit, the holy Spirit, may '... guide our minds with thy blessed light, with love our hearts inflame, and with thy strength which ne'er decays, confirm our mortal frame'. In the words of Fr Nadal, friend and confidant of St Ignatius, 'the heart is the workshop of the Holy Spirit'.

'Do not cast me away from your presence, nor deprive me of your holy spirit.'

We know how weak we are, how liable to fail again and again, but we entreat God that we may never sin so gravely as to be 'cast away from [his] presence', or, more precisely, as to cast ourselves away from his presence. And similarly we pray that we may never be deprived of 'your holy spirit' – which for us means 'your Holy Spirit'.

'Give me again the joy of your help; with a spirit of fervour sustain me, that I may teach transgressors your ways and sinners may return to you.'

With forgiveness there always comes 'joy'. It was a well-known member of the English hierarchy who in his no-nonsense way used to say: 'There's something wrong with you if you like going to Confession, but there's also something wrong with you if you don't feel like jumping for joy afterwards'! But despite the joy of sin forgiven, thanks to God's 'help', we have no illusions: we know that it is only the Spirit that can maintain 'a spirit of fervour' in our hearts to 'sustain' and support us. In the strength of that spirit we may find ourselves in a position where we 'teach transgressors', not so much by words (that might sound too patronising) but by the way we live, the good news of God's mercy and compassion so that they in their turn may pluck up courage to 'return to you'.

LET US PRAY: *We pray, Lord, for the Lenten gift of true repentance for our sins, so that you may blot out our offences and wash away our guilt, and that we, with hearts renewed, may give you worthy service in union with your Son and in the power of the Holy Spirit.*

Passion Sunday

Verses from Psalm 21 appear in the Mass of Passion (Palm) Sunday. Nor is that surprising, for it is a psalm which includes vivid reminders of our Lord's sufferings as well as the first promising glimmers of Easter glory. It might have been composed for the mysterious 'disciple' - his identity is not revealed - whom we meet in the passage from Isaiah (50:4-7). There are three similar passages in the second section of Isaiah and all four are commonly referred to as 'Servant Songs', for they speak of a disciple who is the utterly faithful servant of the Lord, who suffers much without offering resistance and whose sufferings bring light and life to his people.

A key to the interpretation of the 'disciple' is to be found in St Paul's wonderful hymn in his letter to the Philippians (2:6-11), where Jesus is presented as one who though divine was the obedient servant of the Father and 'emptied himself' even to death on a cross, and so it is that he has been exalted and is now recognised by all as Lord.

Finally, today's gospel gives us St Mark's stark account of the sufferings and death of the Lord (Mark 14:1-15:47). Re-echoing phrases of Psalm 21 – the cry of abandonment ('My God, my God, why have you deserted me?'), the mockery of bystanders and the casting of lots for his clothing – it highlights the humanity of Jesus, and yet includes the climactic act of faith of the centurion who acknowledges the Crucified One as 'son of God'.

EASTERTIDE

*This
is the day
which was made
by the Lord:
let us
rejoice*

EASTERTIDE

If Easter Sunday brought us to the
summit of the Church's liturgical year,
we are urged by the liturgy to continue our journey
on the high plateau, so to say, for the next fifty days,
the season of Eastertide culminating in the feast of Pentecost.

Easter Sunday

Today we arrive at the first of the Church's feast days and the pinnacle of the Church's liturgical year, the joyful celebration of the resurrection of our Lord Jesus Christ.

The gospel records (John 20:1-9) how the disciples Peter and John slowly came to the realisation that their Master had truly risen. Up to the moment when they stood in the empty tomb and gazed down upon linen cloths, no longer shrouding his body but lying discarded on the ground, they had simply 'failed to understand ... that he must rise from the dead'.

However, as the first reading (Acts 10:34, 37-43) indicates, Peter was later able to proclaim not simply that God had 'raised [Jesus] to life' but that he and the other disciples had actually 'eaten and drunk with him after his resurrection from the dead'.

Each of the alternative second readings – the one taken from Colossians (3:1-4), the other from 1 Corinthians (5:6-8) – draws practical conclusions for all who, through baptism, share in the resurrection. Their new 'life ... is hidden with Christ in God', and therefore their thoughts must no longer be anchored to this earth, they must rid themselves of 'the old yeast', the old way of life.

And finally all is brought together in Psalm 117, THE Easter psalm above all others. The verses for today's Mass are identical with those used at the Vigil Mass; and there will be many reminders of the psalm throughout the Easter season.

Prayerful Ponderings

'This day was made by the Lord; we rejoice and are glad.'
This sentence, which actually belongs to a later verse in Psalm 117, not only serves as the response to the psalm but also helps to set the tone for today's great feast. In fact it will be used for the Alleluia verse every day throughout the Easter Octave. Again and again we confess that this astounding day, which sees the resurrection of Jesus from the tomb, is the work of God himself. Only he could have brought it about, only he could even have envisaged such a wonder. And we, who only a few days ago were lamenting the death of Jesus, now find ourselves rejoicing and filled with gladness.

'Give thanks to the Lord for he is good, for his love has no end. Let the sons of Israel say: "His love has no end."'
This is the opening verse of the psalm; its first sentence serves also as the psalm's conclusion. This bracketing of the hymn with a call to give thanks not only indicates the nature of the psalm (a thanksgiving) but also suggests that it was originally used in a communal setting. Perhaps it was the occasion of an important individual's solemn entering of the Temple to express his gratitude, perhaps a king returning successfully from battle. But of course on this day of the Lord's own making, we think of the King of kings who by his resurrection has triumphed over every evil force that threatens human happiness. We think and we give thanks, for we know that Easter Sunday provides the clinching proof

of the goodness of our God and of his endless loving mercy. In the psalm all 'the sons of Israel', the whole people, are invited to take up the cry that 'his love has no end'. Today, for even more powerful reasons than Israel's, we are called to give thanks for God's undying love.

'The Lord's right hand has triumphed; his right hand raised me up. I shall not die, I shall live and recount his deeds.'
In the second section of the psalm, the singer speaks of being caught up in a terrible plight and then of the way in which defeat was turned into victory. Only the strong 'right hand' of God, a symbol of his power, could have turned the catastrophe of Good Friday into the triumph of Easter Sunday; it was that hand that 'raised... up' the crucified Christ. And, as St Paul says, 'Christ, having died, dies now no more, death shall no more have power over him'(Romans 6:9). The Risen Christ will never again face death; he lives for ever to 'recount [God's mighty] deeds'.

'The stone which the builders rejected has become the cornerstone. This is the work of the Lord, a marvel in our eyes.'
And finally a wonderful word-picture highlights the incredible contrast between Jesus, disowned and crucified, and Jesus ablaze with resurrection glory. On Good Friday he, God's chosen stone, had been 'rejected' by the 'builders' (the leaders of the people), who regarded him as surplus to their requirements. But on Easter Sunday it becomes clear that God has vindicated the rejected stone, making him 'the cornerstone' or keystone of a new structure, the new people of God. It's fascinating to see how naturally this metaphor of the discarded stone was used in the early Church in reference to Jesus' death and resurrection (Acts 4:11).

LET US PRAY: *Lord God, we are your Easter people; in the resurrection of your Son we 'have been brought back to true life'; and so we pray that, in the power of the Spirit, we may be renewed in mind and heart.*

Second Sunday of Easter

The rejoicing of Easter continues. Every Sunday is a 'little Easter', a celebration of the Lord's resurrection, but that is peculiarly so of the Sundays of Paschaltide.

The first reading (Acts of the Apostles 2:32-37) gives a rather idealised summary of the way life was lived in the first Christian community. Easter faith so fashioned their outlook that they were all 'united, heart and soul' and made sure that 'none of their members was ever in want'. Meanwhile, the apostles, the leaders of the community 'continued to testify to the resurrection of the Lord Jesus.

In today's second reading (1 John 5:1-6), St John boldly declares that Easter faith brings us 'victory over the world' (the world insofar as it is hostile to God). But that faith has practical consequence in terms of love of God and love of our fellow men and women, and will sometimes make stern demands of us. We dare not forget that we are saved by the 'water and blood' that flowed from Christ on Calvary. Washed in water at baptism and nourished by blood in the Eucharist, we are to follow his example.

Today's Gospel (John 20:19-31) recounts the events of the first Sunday after Easter Day. Thomas had been absent when the Risen Lord appeared to the other disciples and gave them the resurrection gift of peace; but now, a week later, Thomas also is granted an appearance of the Lord. It elicits from him the magnificent confession: 'My Lord, and my God', and leads Jesus to assure us that the truly blessed ones are those (like ourselves) 'who have not seen and yet believe'.

Predictably, the responsorial psalm is again taken from psalm 117. We have seen that originally it may have been associated with a king; we use it of the King, our Risen Lord.

Prayerful Ponderings

'Give thanks to the Lord for he is good, for his love has no end'.

As was the case last week, today's response is taken from the opening words of the psalm. However, there is an alternative: the psalmist's words may be replaced by a triple 'Alleluia!'. In either case the sense is much the same: praise and glory and thanksgiving be to our God and to his Son, risen from the dead, for their love which 'has no end'.

'Let the sons of Israel say: "His love has no end". Let the sons of Aaron say: "His love has no end". Let those who fear the Lord say: "His love has no end"'.

This opening litany calls upon all the people to acknowledge that 'his love has no end'. First, the invitation goes out to 'the sons of Israel', the people in general; next to 'the sons of Aaron', the priests; then to 'those who fear the Lord', possibly those who believe in God though they do not belong to the Jewish community; but, finally, on this day the invitation is addressed to us; we too are encouraged to join in the chorus of grateful praise for God's *hesed*, his ever-faithful love.

'The Lord's right hand has triumphed; his right hand raised me up. I shall not die, I shall live and recount his deeds. I was punished, I was punished by the Lord, but not doomed to die'.

We can imagine the risen Jesus joyfully declaring that in his resurrection the 'right hand [of the Father] has triumphed'; it was 'his right hand that raised me up'. In the Hebrew Bible the rescue of Israel was attributed to the strong right hand of God. Now that same hand has achieved an even greater exodus, raising Jesus from the tomb (see Luke 9:31); on Calvary, only a little while ago, it must have seemed that he 'was [being] punished by the Lord', but, if so, the punishment was for our sins. And in fact the punishment was turned into triumph; though 'doomed to die', he lives forever.

'The stone which the builders rejected has become the corner stone. This is the work of the Lord, a marvel in our eyes. This day was made by the Lord; we rejoice and are glad'.

Once more the reversal of fortune between Good Friday and Easter Sunday is vividly presented under the metaphor of a stone 'rejected' by the builders as of no consequence but later singled out as the all-important 'corner stone'. Significantly, Jesus himself had appealed to this very verse to indicate how the leaders of the people would cast him aside (Matthew: 21:42). And once again there is the acknowledgment that this is 'a marvel' which only the Lord could have achieved. Hence, this day is of the Lord's own making or, more simply, it is the Lord's day, for us, as for Christians down through the ages, a day of rejoicing and gladness.

LET US PRAY: *Loving Father, we thank you for the gift of faith in your Beloved Son and in his resurrection from the dead. May that faith be for us a source of strength, an incentive to grow in love and a resolve never to doubt that your strong right hand will always support us.*

Third Sunday of Easter

In a variety of ways, today's readings offer encouragement to us in our sinfulness and weakness of faith. In the first (Acts 3:13-15, 17-19), Peter insists that even those responsible for Christ's death are not without hope: they may well have acted through ignorance rather than malice, and now, with Christ's exaltation, they are called upon to 'repent and turn to God'.

In the second reading (1 John 2:1-5), while urging us to 'stop sinning', John also reminds us that when we do sin 'we have our advocate ... Jesus Christ ... the sacrifice that takes our sins away'.

In the gospel (Luke 24:35-48) the Risen Lord appears to his half-believing friends and bolsters their faith by joining them for a meal, inviting them to 'touch and see' his hands and feet and finally opening their minds to the Scriptures.

The responsorial psalm is made up of excepts from Psalm 4, one of a group of psalms known as songs of confidence. They seem to have originated in the expressions of trust in God which are to be found in virtually all the psalms of petition. In fact some experts would describe this psalm as a lament, a cry for help.

Prayerful Ponderings

'When I call, answer me, O God of justice; from anguish you released me, have mercy and hear me.'

Even while calling upon God for help, the psalmist also expresses confidence that the prayer will be heard. It's a confidence that arises from past experience of being heard, of receiving God's 'mercy', of being released 'from anguish', of being given room to move when hemmed in on every side. The psalmist believes that the same will happen again.

'It is the Lord who grants favours to those whom he loves; the Lord hears me whenever I call him.'

Another bold statement: 'the Lord' will never fail 'those whom he loves', those who have confidence in him. And if at times our faith seems frail and faltering, like that of the apostles in today's gospel, we have only to turn to him in prayer, for 'the Lord hears [us] whenever [we] call him'

'"What can bring us happiness?" many say. Lift up the light of your face on us, O Lord.'

The psalmist rehearses the question on everyone's lips: 'What can bring us happiness?' It was the great question in the psalmist's day; it remains so in our day – and it will remain so till the end of time. Humanity is forever seeking happiness, fulfilment – often enough in the wrong places and the wrong ways, but nonetheless seeking – because that is the way God created us: our hearts are restless until they find that for which they were made. The psalmist not only raises the question, but also provides the answer: 'What can bring us happiness?' I will tell you: only let 'the light of your face', radiant with joy and love, smile upon us, 'O Lord'. (In the following verse, which unfortunately does not appear in today's responsorial psalm, the psalmist says that to have the friendship of our God brings greater joy than 'abundance of corn and new wine' or, as we might say, any amount of material possessions.) Little wonder that the refrain for today's psalm is 'Lift up the light of your face on us, O Lord'.

'I will lie down in peace and sleep comes at once, for you alone, Lord, make me dwell in safety.'
Having professed confidence in the Lord, perhaps at the end of a frenzied day, the psalmist is now ready to 'lie down in peace'; and 'sleep comes at once' in the sure knowledge of being in the safe-keeping of the Lord, who 'alone' enables one to take one's repose 'in safety'. It is the reference to sleep which has made this psalm a popular night prayer (see Night Prayer for Sunday I in the 'Prayer of the Church'). However, it might also be used of the sleep of death; we place our future in the hands of God, confident that even in death we shall 'dwell in safety'.

LET US PRAY: *In a world ablaze with the wonders of science and technology, let us never forget, Lord, that only you and your love can ever satisfy our restless hearts. No matter what life brings, keep our confidence strong and resilient.*

Fourth Sunday of Easter

In today's first reading (Acts 4:8-12) Peter and John, interrogated over a miracle in which they have been involved, declare that the healing came not from themselves but from 'the name of Jesus Christ the Nazarene' and that there is no other name in which 'we can be saved' except that of Jesus, who was cast aside like a stone rejected by builders.

The wonder of that salvation is brought home by St John (1 John 3:1-2) when he declares that we are now called, and actually are, the sons and daughters of God, and we look forward to seeing him 'as he really is' and being transformed into his likeness.

In the gospel (John 10:11-18) Jesus proclaims himself to be our good shepherd who willingly laid down his life on our behalf. His resurrection is proof not only of the Father's enduring love for him but also his enduring love for us, the brothers and sisters of Jesus.

Psalm 117 is the responsorial psalm. We have had excerpts from it before, indeed as recently as Easter Sunday and again on the Second Sunday of Easter. That is not surprising, for it is the thanksgiving prayer of one, probably a king, who, having gone through a great ordeal, has not only been rescued but exalted.

Prayerful Ponderings

'Give thanks to the Lord for he is good, for his love has no end.'
All are invited to raise their voices in praise and to give thanks 'to the Lord for he is good'. We may not know the circumstances in which this song was originally sung, but there is no doubt about its appropriateness for the season of Eastertide. This is the season in which we thank God for all that he has done for us through his Son Jesus Christ, culminating in his resurrection and ascension into glory. The saga of our Lord, the good shepherd who lays down his life for his sheep but has power to take it up again (see today's gospel), is proof beyond doubt that God's steadfast love for us, literally, 'has no end'.

'It is better to take refuge in the Lord than to trust in men: it is better to take refuge in the Lord than to trust in princes.'
Experience has shown – in the original setting of the psalm, it may have been a priest or prophet who delivered this piece of practical wisdom – that reliance upon 'the Lord' is always to be preferred to trusting in human help, even if it be that of 'princes'. Later, Paul will express the same truth in the powerful phrase: 'If God is for us who can be against us?' (Romans 8:31).

'I will thank you for you have given answer and you are my saviour.'

The victorious king is in no doubt about it: his victory is due not simply to his own efforts but, above all, to the fact that his prayers were answered and God proved himself his 'saviour'. Can we not also imagine a song of thanksgiving on the lips of Jesus as he was raised by his Father from the tomb – saved out of the grip of death itself?

'The stone which the builders rejected has become the corner stone. This is the work of the Lord, a marvel in our eyes.'
The first sentence, which is the refrain for today's psalm, may have been a proverbial saying for an unexpected reversal of fate: like a stone 'rejected' by builders as useless but ending up as the keystone of the structure, so is the person (the king) who is rejected but rises to great prominence. In the early Church (see today's first reading, and also Our Lord's own use of it in Mark 12:1-11) it was used as a way of showing how Jesus, though 'rejected', even put to death, by his own people, has through the glory of the resurrection become 'the corner stone', the sure foundation on which the Church is built. Who could doubt that 'this is the work of the Lord'; it is in all truth 'a marvel in our eyes'.

'Blessed in the name of the Lord is he who comes. We bless you from the house of the Lord.'
These words seem to be a greeting to the triumphant king as he arrives at the Temple. In Mark 11:9 they become the joyful cry of the crowd as they welcome Jesus into Jerusalem. And for us today they become, at the *Sanctus* of every Mass, a song of joyous greeting to our crucified and risen Lord: here, in 'the house of the Lord' we praise and 'bless' him.

'I will thank you for you have given answer and you are my saviour. Give thanks to the Lord for he is good; for his love has no end.'

Once again an expression of gratitude for the way that God has 'given answer', has proved himself to be 'saviour'. Now, just as at the beginning of this long psalm, all are invited to join in giving 'thanks to the Lord' for his goodness and never-ending 'love'.

LET US PRAY: *It is with great joy, Lord, that we give thanks to you on this day when we recall that Jesus, once rejected and done to death, has risen again in glory. He is indeed our good shepherd, with power to lay down his life and to take it up again. May we confidently follow him all the days of our life.*

Fifth Sunday of Easter

Just as the whole of the Easter season is a celebration of the paschal mystery, the dying and rising of Jesus, so the readings of today's Mass reveal both the suffering side and the joyous side of Christian living.

In the first reading (Acts 9:26-31) we hear how Paul was accepted, though not without understandable caution, into the Christian community; how some of the Jews resolved to kill him; how having escaped, he preached the good news and how, despite all, he was 'filled with the consolation of the Holy Spirit'.

The gospel (John 15:1-8), with our Lord's wonderful parable of the vine and branches, hints at both suffering (the vine must be pruned) and joy (the vine bearing much fruit).

Christians, says the second reading (1 John 3:18-24), are those who keep the two commandments of believing in Christ and of loving one another; and so they bear 'much fruit'. They may have to suffer for their following of Christ but they still rejoice in the knowledge that he has conquered.

The first two-thirds of Psalm 21 unfold a story of terrible suffering and humiliation, but the final third, which is today's responsorial psalm, recounts how sufferings have been transformed into rejoicing, how defeat has given way to stunning victory.

Prayerful Ponderings

'You, Lord, are my praise in the great assembly.'
This verse is the refrain for today's psalm, though Alleluia may be used as an alternative. Psalms of petition, 'laments', to give them their technical name, usually end with thanksgiving and rejoicing because the prayer has been heard. But the ending of Psalm 21 can only be described as spectacular, so incredible is the reversal of fortunes which it portrays, and so complete is the contrast with the dreadful tale of suffering in earlier verses. The psalmist, standing in the midst of 'the great assembly' of God's people, is filled with praise of the 'Lord'. Shortly that praise will be taken up by an ever-widening circle of worshippers.

'My vows I will pay before those who fear him. The poor shall eat and shall have their fill. They shall praise the Lord, those who seek him. May their hearts live for ever!'
The prayer has been heard when all seemed hopeless. And now 'vows' must be fulfilled in the presence of all 'those who fear him'. The discharge of promises made involves a sacrifice of thanksgiving, followed by a banquet in which 'the poor shall eat and ... have their fill'. At the heart of our Easter celebrations, we have the Eucharist: the re-presentation of the dying and rising of Christ, the sacrifice of thanksgiving, the banquet in which we 'the poor' eat of a Bread which has eternal consequences, for those who eat this bread in faith will indeed 'live for ever'.

'All the earth shall remember and return to the Lord, all families of the nations worship before him. They shall worship him, all the mighty of the earth; before him shall bow all who go down to the dust.'

The thoughts of the psalmist, at least from this point onwards, are so extravagant that they seem to make full sense only in reference to our Risen Lord. What he has done has world-wide repercussions: all the 'earth' remembers (in the biblical sense of recognising that all that he done is a reality affecting them now); it returns, repentant, 'to the Lord'; 'all ... the nations worship before him', from 'the mighty' ones to those 'who go down to the dust' (which probably means the dying but possibly even those already dead).

'And my soul shall live for him, my children serve him. They shall tell of the Lord to generations yet to come, declare his faithfulness to peoples yet unborn: "These things the Lord has done."'

'We know that Christ, being raised from the dead, will never die again; death no longer has dominion over him' (Romans 6:9). He lives for ever to the glory of the Father. And yet, because of his dying and rising, generations 'yet to come', even to the end of time, will 'declare [God's] faithfulness' and 'peoples yet unborn' will rejoice in what 'the Lord has done'. And so this psalm, which began with a fierce cry of dereliction, 'My God, my God, why have you forsaken me?', now ends with a triumphant cry of victory: Good Friday has given way to Easter Sunday.

LET US PRAY: *Lord God, reflecting on the passion and death of Jesus, we pray that we may have courage to follow him always, confident that beyond all the demands and pains of Christian living there lies the promise of our ultimate sharing in his triumph.*

Sixth Sunday of Easter

The central theme of today's readings is God's unfailing love. We hear how the Holy Spirit, God's love personified, overrides human plans and categories, making it clear that the Church's mission is for the whole human race - Gentiles as well as Jews (Acts 10:25-26, 34-35, 44-48).

The second reading (1 John 4:7-10) provides the nearest thing to a definition of God to be found in Old Testament or New: quite simply, 'God is love'.

In Jesus the love of God has been made manifest, for he loves us as he is loved by the Father. He has laid down his life for us, so making it possible for us to become his friends and to share in the intimate unity that exists between himself and his Father, but also challenging us 'to go out and bear fruit' by observing the commandment to love one another 'as I have loved you' (John 15:9-17).

Psalm 97, though only a brief excerpt from it appears in today's responsorial psalm, sings with joy of the wonder worked by the Lord in achieving universal salvation.

Prayerful Ponderings

'Sing a new song to the Lord for he has worked wonders. His right hand and his holy arm have brought salvation.'
The psalm opens with an invitation to raise our voices in 'song' in order to celebrate the 'wonders' that the Lord 'has worked'. It is called a 'new' song because it arises from the new situation brought about by the saving work of God. 'His right hand and his holy arm' conjure up a picture of God as a powerful warrior, who overcomes all his enemies by his might. Probably the psalmist had the Exodus, or the return from Babylon, in mind. But for us the psalm serves as a reminder of the greater wonders achieved through Jesus Christ. He is not a mighty warrior but a victim of crucifixion; yet God has raised him from the dead and exalted him to his right hand. Through his death and resurrection he has won 'salvation' for all the nations – he has brought into existence a totally new situation in which we can call upon God as Abba (dear Father).

'The Lord has made known his salvation; has shown his justice to the nations. He has remembered his truth and love for the house of Israel.'
The refrain for today's responsorial psalm - unless Alleluia (= Praise God) is chosen as a substitute - is a slightly shortened version of the first sentence of this verse. It stresses the fact that God has revealed 'to the nations', to all the world (see first reading), his saving power

and his 'justice', his righteousness. But, as the second sentence makes clear, he has also revealed his 'love' and faithfulness to 'the house of Israel'. This psalm, like so many others, seems to visualise, and long for, a time when the royal dignity of God will be manifested more clearly than ever before. In the events we celebrate during this Easter season, we see how the longings of Israel have been realised and the Lord's faithfulness to his people honoured: the outstretched arms of Jesus on the cross offer an embrace of love to the whole human race.

'All the ends of the earth have seen the salvation of our God. Shout to the Lord all the earth, ring out your joy.'
Once more, the statement is made that all humanity, 'all the ends of the earth', have witnessed 'the salvation of God', and so all are invited to 'shout' and 'ring out [their] joy'. As we respond to that invitation, we can perhaps imagine the joy that filled Cornelius' heart when he was admitted into the community of the faithful (see first reading); but we dare not forget that we, who have learned how God has shown his love to the world, are summoned to reveal that love to others in our daily lives.

LET US PRAY: *In the face of your overwhelming love for us, Lord God, we beg you to help us so that despite our human weaknesses we may witness to that love in the way we treat our sisters and brothers, and so may others be brought to join in the 'new song' of rejoicing.*

Seventh Sunday of Easter

On this, the Sunday sandwiched between Ascension Day and Pentecost, the readings reflect the astonishing story of how events taking place in a tiny Roman province in the Middle East led to the establishment of a kingdom of love which has spread to the ends of the earth. This story is already hinted at in the responsorial psalm - taken from Psalm 102 - which describes God's love in terms of the height, depth and breadth of the universe.

In the first reading (Acts 1:15-17, 20-26) we see how a replacement is found for Judas; in this way the group of twelve apostles, representing the twelve tribes of the new Israel as well as the universality of the Church's mission, is once more complete. Through the ministry of the Christian community God's love will be 'made flesh' in the world.

John, in the second reading (1 John 4:11-16), returns to the theme of God's love for us and our need, as a consequence, to respond by faith and love, both gifts of the Holy Spirit.

On the threshold of his return to the Father, Jesus prays for his disciples (John 17:11-19) that they may be kept true to his name, and that they and their followers will be united in faith and love so that they may reflect that life of mutual love which is the Trinity.

Prayerful Ponderings

'My soul, give thanks to the Lord; all my being, bless his holy name.'
In the face of God's unconditional and unmerited love, we cannot but be filled with bewilderment and gratitude. St Catherine of Siena remarked that though God clearly has no need of us, yet it seems that he's so madly in love with us that he cannot live without us. That is why he created us, and then redeemed us. The psalmist addresses 'my soul', urging it to 'give thanks'. What that means becomes clear when the word 'soul' is replaced by the phrase 'all my being'. It is not just one part of us, however noble, but everything that is in us that instinctively longs to respond to God's overwhelming love.

'My soul, give thanks to the Lord and never forget all his blessings.'
Once more 'my soul', my whole being, is exhorted to 'give thanks'. One of our greatest dangers is forgetfulness, in the sense that we so easily take things for granted. And so the psalmist seems to be encouraging us to 'count our blessings one by one', to recall the innumerable signs of God's love in our own life and the lives of those who are dear to us, above all the fact that he has loved us into existence and loved us into a sharing in his own divine life.

'For as the heavens are high above the earth so strong is his love for those who fear him.'

This sentence seems to suggest that the psalmist is almost lost for words in the attempt to describe the power and the extent of God's love. Let's put it like this, the psalmist seems to say, just think of the distance between this 'earth' and 'the heavens' above us. That will give you some idea of how great and how 'strong is his love'. It is a love that goes out to all his creatures without exception, though it is 'those who fear him', who revere him for what he is, who are most keenly aware of his goodness and most open to experience its effects.

'As far as the east is from the west so far does he remove our sins.'
This time, in trying to explain the generosity of God's forgiveness, the psalmist turns to geography. Think of the furthest point 'east' you can go, the psalmist suggests, and then of the furthest point 'west'; that will give you some idea of how far God removes 'our sins'. God's forgiveness, an aspect of his love, knows no bounds, not only in the sense that it pardons every repented sin but also in the sense that it removes the sin completely or, perhaps better, it turns even our sins to good (see Romans 8:28) rather in the way that a broken limb, once mended, becomes stronger than ever.

'The Lord has set his sway in heaven and his kingdom is ruling over all. Give thanks to the Lord, all his angels, mighty in power, fulfilling his word.'
Now our attention is switched to 'heaven' and we are reminded of the universality of his rule (of love) which extends not only throughout the world but also throughout the heavenly 'kingdom'. And so, just as the psalm began with a call to us to praise God, so it ends with a call to the angels, 'mighty in power' and always obedient to 'his word', to join us in praise.

LET US PRAY: *Help us, Lord, not only to know with our minds but also to appreciate with our hearts the boundless extent of your love and the incredible generosity of your forgiveness; and so may we desire to love and serve you all the days of our life.*

Pentecost

Today marks the end or, better, the climax of the Great Fifty Days of Eastertide. The coming of the Holy Spirit, and with it the birth of the Church, completes the redeeming work of Christ.

The first reading (Acts 2:1-11) re-tells the story of what happened on the first Pentecost day. The advent of the Spirit was like a new creation, the Church was born and the estrangement of the tower of Babel reversed as the disciples, now filled with the Spirit, discovered that what they said was understood by all their hearers, though they were of different races and different languages.

(The second reading and the gospel for this Sunday of Year B are the same as those for the corresponding Sunday of Year A. However, the missal offers alternatives and, for those who choose the optional readings, the following brief comments may prove helpful).

In Galatians 5:16-25 Paul compares the frightful consequences of 'self-indulgence' with the beautiful fruits of the Holy Spirit – love, joy, peace, patience, etc; and ends with the plea that we 'be directed by the Spirit'

In the gospel (John 15:26-27; 16:12-15) Jesus promises that the Holy Spirit will come and continue to witness to him; and those who have been with him since the beginning must witness to him also. If that seems a daunting mission, Jesus assures them that the Spirit of truth will lead them into 'complete truth'.

The author of psalm 103 - in today's Mass we have only a few excerpts from it - is not only a person of deep faith, one who sees that nature bears the finger-prints of its Maker and is kept in being by his Spirit, but also a poet who knows how to use language to celebrate what he sees. It reads like a poetical version of the creation account in Genesis 1.

Prayerful Ponderings

'Bless the Lord, my soul! Lord God, how great you are! How many are your works, O Lord! The earth is full of your riches.' As you hear these words, you can almost imagine the poet standing beside the Creator as he gazes upon his work of creation and sees that it is good, very good. The psalmist gasps with wonder and delight: 'Lord God, how great you are!' The whole world seems to be alive with his masterpieces. He bids his 'soul' to bless the Lord, as though he wants his innermost deepest self to be involved in the wonder and the worship. On this day we are invited to share the psalmist's praise, remembering however that the Holy Spirit has worked a new and even more wonderful creation, in which we are enabled to call upon God as Abba (dear Father).

'You take back your spirit, they die, returning to the dust from which they came. You send forth your spirit, they are created; and you renew the faced of the earth.' After reflecting on the countless creatures God had made, the psalmist marvels at the way he has provided for them all: their very 'spirit' (the Hebrew words also means 'breath) comes as gift from God; should he take it away, 'they die'; should he restore it again, 'they are created' and the whole of creation is renewed. A slightly amended form of this verse, making it into a prayer that God will send forth 'your Spirit (spelt with a capital 'S') and renew the face of the earth', is the refrain for today's responsorial psalm; we are surely meant to realise that if we give thanks to God for the gift of our life's breath, still more must we thank him that, through the gift of the Holy Spirit, he shares his own life with us: we are indeed renewed and transformed.

'May the glory of the Lord last for ever! May the Lord rejoice in his works!'

These words come from towards the end of the psalm. It is as though the psalmist is almost lost for words and can only say that he or she wants the Lord's 'glory' to go on and on for ever and at the same time wants the Lord to go on rejoicing in all 'his works'.

'May my thoughts be pleasing to him. I find my joy in the Lord'.

Finally, the plea that the psalmist's own 'thoughts', the psalmist's meditation, all that has been said in this psalm, may be like a 'pleasing' offering to the Lord. It is 'in the Lord' that the psalmist (and we too) find our best and lasting 'joy.'

LET US PRAY: *Creator God, who make all things new, come and, on this day of Pentecost, breathe your Holy Spirit into us anew so that we may work with you for the renewal of the whole world.*

The Most Holy Trinity

A week ago the feast of Pentecost brought the season of Eastertide to an end, but before we return to the Ordinary Sundays in the Year, we celebrate the feast of the Most Holy Trinity, which takes us to the heart of our faith and the source of all liturgical celebrations.

Though in Old Testament times there was no awareness of the doctrine of the Trinity, today's reading from Deuteronomy (4:32-34, 39-40) shows how firmly Israel expressed its belief in the oneness of God and his superiority over all the so-called deities of surrounding nations.

In today's gospel (Matthew 28:16-20), Jesus commissions his disciples to take his message to all nations: and part of that message is that new Christians are to be baptised in the name of God who is Father, Son and Holy Spirit.

Even before the Gospels were written, Paul was teaching that the Spirit dwells in our hearts enabling us to acknowledge God as 'Abba, Father' and become co-heirs with Jesus Christ, the Father's only Son (Romans 8:14-17).

The verses selected from Psalm 32 for today's responsorial psalm speak of the power of God's word but also of the tenderness he shows to those who reverence him.

Prayerful Ponderings

'Happy the people the Lord has chosen as his own.'
The refrain of today's psalm is in the form of a beatitude: 'O the happiness' of those who belong to God's people, sings the psalmist. But happier still are those who, like ourselves, have been baptised in the name of Father, Son and Holy Spirit, who have been 'chosen [by the Lord] as his own'.

'The word of the Lord is faithful and all his works to be trusted. The Lord loves justice and right and fills the earth with his love.'
The psalmist shares Moses' awesome respect for God's word: 'Was there ever a word so majestic?' (first reading). They have complete confidence in his covenant faithfulness; they are confident that he is always loyal, that his 'word' is 'faithful', that everything he says is 'to be trusted'. We too, the children of the new covenant, have absolute confidence in God's word and in that of his Son, Jesus, who assured us that 'Heaven and earth will pass away, but my words will not pass away' (Matthew 24:35). His faithfulness is an aspect of his love for 'justice and right'. Indeed, the psalmist declares, he 'fills the earth with his love'. In a way that the psalmist could never understand, we know that God is Trinity, a community of love, and that all that is in this world can be seen as an outpouring of that love.

'By his word the heavens were made, by the breath of his mouth all the stars. He spoke; and they came to be. He commanded; they sprang into being.'

God's 'word' is not only reliable, it is also creative. When we hear of God's making 'the heavens' by his word, and 'the stars' of heaven 'by the breath of his mouth', our thoughts turn to the first page of the Bible where our Creator God is revealed as One who brings all things into existence effortlessly at his word. He simply 'spoke; and they came to be', 'commanded; [and] they sprang into being'. But today we celebrate an even greater revelation: that this Creator God is also Trinity, is Father, Son and Holy Spirit.

'The Lord looks on those who revere him, on those who hope in his love, to rescue their souls from death, to keep them alive in famine.'

The doctrine of the Trinity is a powerful statement of the utter transcendence of God, yet this verse reminds us that despite (or because of) his greatness, he 'looks' with loving kindness 'on those who revere him'. The proof of this shines out above all in the fact that Jesus is God-with-us 'until the end of time' (gospel) and that through the gift of the Spirit we have all come to share in his divine Sonship (second reading). We are confident that just as he saves us from spiritual 'famine', especially through his word and through the Eucharist, so also at the end he will 'rescue [our] souls from death' and draw us into the face-to-face vision of our Three-Personed God.

'Our soul is waiting for the Lord. The Lord is our help and our shield. May your love be upon us, O Lord, as we place all our hope in you'

We acknowledge that 'the Lord is our help and our shield'; that is why we are always 'waiting' for him, knowing that he will never desert us. And so today's psalm ends with a prayer which is at once a request and an affirmation of trust: 'May your love be upon us ... as we place all our hope in you.'

LET US PRAY: *Praise to the Father, who created us; praise to the Son, who redeemed us and commissioned us to spread the good news; praise to the Holy Spirit who sanctified us, making us into sons and daughters of God; praise be to the Most Holy Trinity now and for ever.*

ORDINARY TIME

*Let
my prayer
rise
like incense
before
you*

ORDINARY TIME

*Ordinary Time is the liturgical period
stretching from after Christmastide
until Lent, and then from the Sunday
after Pentecost up to, and including,
the feast of Christ the King.*

Second Sunday in Ordinary Time

'Ordinary' time is that part of the Church's year which falls outside Advent/Christmas, and Lent/Easter and so celebrates the whole mystery of Christ rather than a particular aspect of it. Nonetheless, Ordinary Time begins with the feast of the Baptism of the Lord; that is why this Sunday is called the Second Sunday of Ordinary Time.

The first reading (1 Samuel 3:3-10,19) tells the delightful story of young Samuel, who despite his tender years is so obedient, above all to the Lord. On this Sunday especially, when the responsorial psalm speaks so powerfully of devotion to God's will, we might try to make our own Samuel's prayer: "Speak, Lord, your servant is listening'.

Writing to people in a city notorious for its vice – perhaps our own world is not much better - Paul does not hesitate to proclaim that sins of fornication are utterly opposed to God's will, that consorting with a prostitute in a sense involves Christ himself, since we are with him one body (1 Corinthians 6:13-15,17-20). He reminds them (and us) that they have been 'bought and paid for' by Christ at a great price; therefore, they should use their bodies 'for the glory of God'.

In the gospel (John 1:35-42) John the Baptist recognises in Jesus 'the lamb of God who takes away the sin of the world'; his words so impress his disciples that two of them follow Jesus and so fall under his spell that they willingly spend that day with him – the beginning of a life-time's friendship.

Psalm 39 is the prayer of an individual who has been extricated from dreadful straights, which he describes – though the words do not appear in the extract of the psalm we hear today – as a 'deadly pit', and he now comes to the Temple to give thanks and to express his desire to follow God's will. It's a psalm which voices the frame of mind of our Saviour who, from the moment he came into this world, delighted to do his Father's will and so was able to offer the perfect sacrifice of thanks and praise.

Prayerful Ponderings

'I waited, I waited for the Lord and he stooped down to me; he heard my cry'.

At the heart of all prayer is waiting upon God, simply being there in his presence. But the wonderful news is, as Isaiah the prophet says, that God is waiting for us, too: 'The Lord waits to be gracious to you ... blessed are all those who wait for him'(30:17f). It's an experience that the psalmist has known: prayer was heard and God 'stooped down to me' and rescued me from his 'pit'.

'He put a new song in to my mouth, praise of our God'.

'A life of faith' wrote Henri Nouwen 'is a life of gratitude'. Most of us tend to be more adept at asking than thanking; requests come to our lips rather more readily than does the 'new song' of thanksgiving. The psalmist is in no doubt that even gratitude is not of his own making but comes as gift from God. It's a gift for which we ought to pray.

'In the scroll of the book it stands written that I should do your will'.

The 'scroll of the book' probably refers to the Bible which is the revelation of God's will. The psalmist recognises this and is going to make it the compass by which the whole of life will be directed. There is no more practical way of showing our gratitude to God than by readiness to do his will.

'You do not ask for sacrifice and offerings, but an open ear. Instead, here am I. My God, I delight in your law in the depth of my heart'.

In biblical times it was usual to express thanks to God by offering a bloody animal sacrifice, but the psalmist sees a nobler way - the sacrifice of mind and heart to the will of God. It was our Lord's total dedication to his Father's will that ultimately led to Calvary and to the sacrifice which is the most perfect act of worship the world has ever seen. In the letter to the Hebrews, Jesus is depicted as reciting the words of this verse as he comes into the world. It goes on to declare that he has abolished the old-style sacrifices to replace them with his own: the sacrifice which he once offered, with the shedding of his life's blood, on Calvary and which is re-presented for us in a bloodless manner at every Mass.

'Your justice I have proclaimed in the great assembly. My lips I have not sealed; you know it, O Lord'.
'The great assembly' suggests a festival time when great crowds converged on the Temple. There the psalmist boldly bore testimony to the goodness of God, proclaimed it publicly. And we too need the Sunday gathering at Mass to proclaim our gratitude, in company with our brothers and sisters: it is our Eucharist, our great act of thanks.

'Here I am, O Lord! I come to do your will'
These words which serve as the response to the psalm are also its high point. As already mentioned, we are to think of them first of all as on the lips of Jesus; however, our earnest prayer must surely be that in some measure at least we may make them our own.

LET US PRAY: *We rejoice, Lord, in the realisation that as we wait upon you, you are always waiting for us, waiting to stoop down to us in all our needs. Keep us sensitive to the goodness you show us, make us joyful participants in the thanksgiving of the Mass and help us always to make your will the compass of our lives.*

Third Sunday in Ordinary Time

The first reading (Jonah 3:1-5, 10) tells how God sent his reluctant prophet Jonah to call the pagans of Nineveh to repentance. The attitudes of the Jewish people may have been exclusive, but clearly God's concern and his offer of grace know no bounds.

The Ninevites had their moment of opportunity; in the gospel (Mark 1:14-20), we hear of another moment of opportunity. Jesus announces that 'The time has come'. The reign of God is at hand: repentance and faith are called for. Following him in faith, his new disciples will in their turn gather other followers to Christ.

Paul, in the second reading (1 Corinthians 7:29-31), suggests that another moment of opportunity, the day of the Lord's return, may be closer than we imagine, and so now is the time for us to struggle free of undue concern with the passing events of this life.

The responsorial psalm, which comes from Psalm 24, pleads that God may remember his mercy and we may know his ways.

Prayerful Ponderings

'Lord, make me know your ways. Lord, teach me your paths.'
In view of the other readings, with their suggestion that we should be ready for moments of opportunity, it is hardly surprising that our initial prayer – and the refrain of today's psalm – should be a plea that we may 'know your ways'. In fact, though the psalm includes many requests, the dominant one is for instruction. We long to be taught by the Lord so that we may know 'your paths' – and walk in them.

'Make me walk in your truth, and teach me: for you are God my saviour.'
The plea for instruction continues; we even need to be taught what we already know, in the sense that we need to come to a new and deeper appreciation of it. We ask that God himself may be our teacher and that we may 'walk in your truth'. It's a request that we make with confidence because we know that 'God' is '[our] saviour', he is on our side, he will listen to us.

'Remember your mercy, Lord, and the love you have shown from of old. In your love remember me, because of your goodness, O Lord.'
Interwoven with requests for help are affirmations of trust in the Lord. We trust in his 'mercy', which, as today's readings remind us,

knows no bounds: it extends to everyone, even the Ninevites. Above all, we trust in that steadfast 'love' of his which has shown itself in so many ways 'from of old', in the covenant love of his people, but supremely in the life and death of Jesus Christ our Lord. And finally we trust in his concern for us as individuals, and so we boldly ask him out of his 'goodness' to 'remember me'.

'The Lord is good and upright. He shows the path to those who stray, he guides the humble in the right path; he teaches his way to the poor.'

God is acknowledged to be both 'good' and 'upright'. He is good in himself; he is upright in all his dealings with us. It is significant that the psalm pinpoints his attitude towards 'those who stray', 'the humble' and 'the poor', the very groups to whom Jesus himself was so committed; indeed, it was for that reason that the Pharisees mocked him as 'a friend of sinners' (Luke 15:2). If we have heard his call to repentance in today's gospel, then we should be eager to ask him to help us – who stray so often, who are spiritually poor and needy. We should beg him to show us 'the path', to 'guide' us in it and to 'teach' us to walk always in 'his way'.

LET US PRAY: *Lord, may we respond to your call to repentance and so may we walk in your ways and experience the presence of your reign in our lives.*

Fourth Sunday in Ordinary Time

A key to today's readings is to be found in the refrain of today's responsorial psalm (Psalm 94) where we are bidden to 'listen to his voice' and 'harden not your hearts'.

Moses (Deuteronomy 18:15-20) assured the people that God would send 'a prophet like myself' and would place on his lips God's own words.

That prophet is Jesus Christ, our Lord; he is himself the very Word of God. In the synagogue at Capernaum he speaks with an authority that makes a deep impression, an authority confirmed by a miraculous cure, an authority that calls for our undivided attention (Mark 1:21-28).

There is a sense in which Paul's primary concern (1 Corinthians 7:32-35) is to ensure that we are able to listen with an undivided heart. Believing that the end of the world is at hand, he exhorts people to shun anything that would distract them from listening attentively to the Lord, even marriage if in fact it was felt to be a distraction from the one thing that matters.

Prayerful Ponderings

'Come, ring out our joy to the Lord; hail the rock who saves us. Let us come before him, giving thanks, with songs let us hail the Lord.'

We can imagine a priest or some other official standing at the gates of the Temple, and, as groups approach, inviting them to join him in a prayer of praise. There is no escaping the sense of joyful celebration that pervades the invitation. Significantly, it is with the same invitation that the official Prayer of the Church begins each day; it as though the Church, in asking us to join in the prayer that is resounding throughout the world, is reminding us that to 'hail' our God - the solid 'rock' on whom we depend, the One who 'saves us' and brings us new life - is not simply a duty but also a joy. How fitting that we should 'come before him' with 'songs' on our lips and with a spirit of 'thanks' in our hearts.

'Come in; let us kneel and bend low; let us kneel before the God who made us for he is our God and we the people who belong to his pasture, the flock that is led by his hand.'

We are invited to 'come in', to enter the presence of the Lord; and then to 'bend low' and to 'kneel'. Each of the words - bend low and kneel - carries with it the notion of prostrating oneself, making oneself small (in the way that Muslims do as they bow down at prayer). An act of homage, even though it takes place within the privacy of our own hearts, is an acknowledgement both of who we are and who the Lord is. Yet, though 'he is our God' and we are merely his creatures, the psalm suggests that the relationship between us is close and intimate. He is like a shepherd with a personal care for each of us, 'the people who belong to his pasture'. It ought to leave us with an abiding sense of wonder that 'he is our God' and that we are 'led by his hand'.

'O that today you would listen to his voice!'

The reflections above serve as a preparation for this verse. It is addressed to us ('you') who pray this psalm 'today', in the form of a hope, a deep desire ('O that...!'), that we will 'listen to his voice'. Such listening, which implies the response of obedience, is an essential part of worship: worship cannot be genuine if it does not involve at least a desire to obey 'his voice'. Listening, as we have seen, is a central theme of today's readings.

'Harden not your hearts as at Meribah, as on that day at Massah in the desert when your fathers put me to the test; when they tried me, though they saw my work.'

An important value of the Scriptures is that they often remind us to learn from past history. In this verse we are asked to learn from two places 'Meribah' (= dispute) and 'Massah' (= testing) and what happened there. They were the places where Israel rebelled against the Lord, even queried whether he was still with them. Together they summarise the unbelieving spirit of the people as they trudged through 'the desert' to the promised land (see Exodus 17:1-7). They 'tried' God, put him to the test, even though they had abundant evidence of '[his] work' in the Exodus. In the light of their failure, we are urged not to 'harden [our] hearts', but to keep them receptive to the voice of the Lord, trusting him instinctively because in the life, death and resurrection of Jesus we have seen the mightiest 'work' of God.

LET US PRAY: *As we make our journey through 'this valley of tears', we sometimes find it difficult to believe that we are the object of the loving care of you, our good shepherd. We pray, Lord, that you will not allow us to harden our hearts, but rather will make us ever attentive to your voice and ever ready to respond.*

Fifth Sunday in Ordinary Time

Today we are introduced to Job (7:1-4, 6-7), the perfect example of a good man who is grievously tried by suffering and ill fortune. Despite his obvious bewilderment, he does not cease to cry out to God in prayer.

Job's bewilderment is the keener because he believes that God is the one who 'heals the broken-hearted'. It is a belief proclaimed by Psalm 146, the responsorial psalm for today.

In the gospel (Mark 1:29-39) Jesus reveals God's compassion for the sick, the suffering, the broken-hearted, as he brings healing by his miracles.

Just as Jesus took on himself the 'weakness' of our humanity in order to bring us the compassion of God, so Paul (1 Corinthians 9:16-19, 22-23) describes how he too, 'for the sake of the gospel', has willingly accepted weakness, has chosen to become 'the slave of everyone'

Prayerful Ponderings

'Praise the Lord for he is good; sing to our God for he is loving: to him our praise is due.'
Though we may have known nights when we thought the day would never come (see first reading) and though our sufferings might seem as undeserved as those of Job, today's psalm courageously invites us to 'praise the Lord' and to 'sing' to him. Why? First, because, despite everything, 'he is good'; secondly, because 'he is loving': again, despite everything, he cares for us, has our interests at heart; thirdly, because praise is a debt we owe God as our Creator: it is our 'due'. A possible translation of this verse (see NRSV) would run: 'How good it is to sing praises to our God'. In other words, the psalmist suggests that to praise him is not so much a debt as a delight.

'The Lord builds up Jerusalem and brings back Israel's exiles, he heals the broken-hearted, he binds up all their wounds.'
It seems clear that this psalm was composed after the Lord had brought 'back Israel's exiles' and after the rebuilding of 'Jerusalem' had begun. That restoration, the psalmist seems to suggest, provides a special reason for praising him; it involves the healing of broken hearts and the binding up of 'all their wounds'. Indeed, the refrain of the psalm explicitly links the healing work of God with praise: 'Praise the Lord who heals the broken-hearted'. Our thoughts as

Christians turn to the still more wonderful rescue operation mounted by the Lord Jesus to bring us back from the exile of sin. And we can scarcely hear the refrain, without recalling how he revealed the compassionate concern of the Father for the broken-hearted, especially by his many miracles of healing.

'He fixes the number of the stars; he calls each one by its name. Our Lord is great and almighty; his wisdom can never be measured. The Lord raises the lowly; he humbles the wicked to the dust.'

Having shown that God is deserving of praise for his restoration of Israel, the psalmist adds that he is also deserving of praise because he controls 'the stars' – even though people in nearby countries looked upon the same stars as divine beings. He can actually 'number' them, and not only that: God 'calls each one by its name' and so shows that his authority over them is complete. In all truth, he is 'great', he is 'almighty': just as he can bring back exiled people, so he can (and ultimately will) raise 'the lowly' and humble the proud; and 'his wisdom' is boundless. Yet, as the refrain constantly reminds us, this mighty, all-powerful, all-wise God, the God of Israel and the God of the stars is also the God who heals the broken-hearted and binds up all their wounds. As one commentator notes: 'it turns upside down the familiar argument that in so great a universe our small affairs are too minute to notice' (Derek Kidner).

LET US PRAY: *We remember before you, Lord our God, all those who suffer, especially those whose pain is undeserved and whose faith in you is sorely tested. In their anguish, give them courage to cling to you in abiding trust.*

Sixth Sunday in Ordinary Time

In days gone by leprosy was among the most dreaded of diseases: it was often thought to be contagious and incurable. In Israel there were detailed instructions (some of them are mentioned in the first reading) as to how lepers were to be treated; they were to be socially ostracised for the sake of the community (Leviticus 13:1-2, 44-46).

In the gospel (Mark 1:40-45) we see how Jesus breaks through the taboo about dealings with lepers. Not only does he stretch out his hand and touch the stricken man who kneels before him: he heals him and so restores him to normal living.

In the verses chosen from Psalm 31 to form today's responsorial psalm, we hear of the joy experienced by those whose sins are forgiven. Psalm 31 is one of a group - the others are 6, 37, 50, 101, 129 and 142 - which, from early times in the Church's history, have been known as the 'Penitential Psalms' because of their focus on sin and forgiveness.

St Paul (1 Corinthians 10:31-11:1) urges us to take Christ for our model: in the light of today's gospel that means that we are to reach out in practical concern to the outcasts of our society. Moreover, in the light of the psalm we are to see sin as the principal evil that afflicts ourselves and our world, and therefore we must fight against it 'for the glory of God'.

Prayerful Ponderings

'You are my refuge, O Lord; you fill me with the joy of salvation.'

If sin is the most terrible and harmful of all evils, this refrain serves as a constant reminder that in God there is a 'refuge' for us, a place where we can escape, at least from our own sins. It is in him, and him alone, that we can find forgiveness and, with that, the 'joy of salvation'.

'Happy the man whose offence is forgiven, whose sin is remitted. O happy the man to whom the Lord imputes no guilt, in whose spirit is no guilt.'

The three words – 'offence', 'sin' and 'guilt' – which were used in Psalm 50 reappear in this psalm. They suggest that all sin is a rebellion against God, a waywardness akin to that of an arrow missing its target and a form of crookedness or malformation. As we have seen, leprosy has long been regarded as a natural symbol for sin, though of course sin is more to be feared than any disease. Because of the awful nature of sin, the remission of sin is always a cause for rejoicing. And so, as the psalm says, 'happy' and 'O happy' again is the person 'whose sin is remitted'.

'But now I have acknowledged my sins; my guilt I did not hide. I said: "I will confess my offence to the Lord." And you,

Lord, have forgiven the guilt of my sin.'

Once more 'sin', 'guilt' and 'offence' make their appearance. In a verse which unfortunately does not appear in today's responsorial psalm, the psalmist admits that at first he 'kept ... secret' his sinfulness, or, as we might say, didn't face up to it, even though it caused him a good deal of heartache and suffering. 'But now' things have changed completely, because sin has been 'acknowledged'; the psalmist has made the decision: 'I will confess to the Lord'. 'And you, Lord' - the emphasis is on the 'you' - 'have forgiven'. The psalmist is expressing a sense of relief akin perhaps to that which the Sacrament of Reconciliation brings to so many people.

'Rejoice, rejoice in the Lord, exult you just! O come, ring out your joy, all you upright of heart.'

These are the final words of the psalm - several verses have been omitted - but they sum up the emotions of the psalmist (and of ourselves?) as we reflect on the forgiveness of our God. There is a great desire that all the 'just', 'all you upright of heart', might 'rejoice', 'exult' and 'ring out your joy'. Perhaps it will come as no surprise to learn that St Augustine had this psalm inscribed on the wall above his bed. He could begin each new day with the assurance that God never ceases to give us the opportunity to begin again, no matter what our sins may be.

LET US PRAY: *Lord God, in forgiving our sins you show not only your love but also your power. We, who so often find ourselves caught in the trammels of sin, give you thanks for the abundance of your compassion and the unwearied patience of your love.*

Seventh Sunday in Ordinary Time

The 'new deed' which God is to perform, according to Isaiah (43:18-19, 21-22, 24-25), is the liberation of his people from exile, but with it goes a liberation still more wonderful: he will 'blot out everything and not remember [their] sins'.

Jesus is accused of blasphemy when he claims the divine prerogative of forgiving sins, but substantiates the claim by a miracle of healing (Mark 2:1-12).

Paul (2 Corinthians 1:18-22) assures us that in Christ we have an expression of the fidelity of God. We have 'our standing' in him; and in the Holy Spirit we have a pledge that God will rescue us from our sins

The responsorial psalm (Psalm 40) is in the form of a thanksgiving for healing, above all for the healing of our sins.

Prayerful Ponderings

'Happy the man who considers the poor and the weak.'
The psalm begins, as Our Lord's Sermon on the Mount begins (see Matthew 5:3), with a beatitude: 'happy' - or, better, 'blessed': something more than a superficial jollity - is the person who shows practical concern for 'the poor and the weak'. There are more than twenty such beatitudes in the course of the Psalter and almost always they appear, as in this case, in a context of instruction. We who pray this psalm are being gently instructed to review our own attitudes towards those on the margins of society. The Millennium Prayer used in the Liverpool Archdiocese contains a sentence which might have been inspired by this verse: in the Lord's kingdom, it says, 'the weakest members are not disposable but indispensable'. Is that how we regard them?

'The Lord will save him in the day of evil, will guard him, give him life, make him happy in the land and will not give him up to the will of his foes. The Lord will help him on his bed of pain, he will bring him back from sickness to health.'
Those who take to heart the instruction given in the previous verse may count upon the blessings which the psalmist now describes: the Lord will 'save' them when times are hard, will 'guard' and protect them, will give them 'life' and happiness, and will not allow their 'foes' to get the better of them; when they are sick or in 'pain',

he will restore them to health. In fact those who care for 'the poor and the weak' do not always receive such blessings, at least on this side of the grave, despite the psalmist's promise; it might therefore be more helpful (and the original Hebrew could be understood this way) to take this verse as a prayer rather than a statement of fact: 'May the Lord save them, guard them, etc.'

'As for me, I said: "Lord, have mercy on me, heal my soul for I have sinned against you.'
At this point the psalm links up with the main theme of today's readings. This verse, or at any rate the second part of it, forms the refrain for the responsorial psalm. Recognising, on the one hand, the fact of personal sinfulness, and, on the other, the fact that God's greatest blessing is to show 'mercy', the psalmist humbly confesses: 'I have sinned against you', and pleads 'have mercy on me, heal my soul'. We, who are able to join the psalmist in confession of sin, are obviously meant to join the psalmist in the plea for forgiveness and healing.

'If you uphold me I shall be unharmed and set in your presence for evermore.'
There is enormous encouragement in the certainty that so long as God upholds us, keeps us secure, frees us from our sins, we shall never come to any real and lasting harm. As mentioned earlier, even if we show concern for the poor and needy, we may not enjoy all those blessings the psalmist spoke of, but, on the assurance of the Lord himself (see Matthew 25), we can humbly look forward to enjoying his 'presence for evermore' - the reward of eternal happiness.

'Blessed be the Lord, the God of Israel from age to age. Amen. Amen.'

The Psalter is divided into five books, perhaps following the pattern of the Torah, the first five books of the Bible. Each of them ends with an outburst of praise, usually followed by a double 'Amen'. This verse, in fact, marks the end of the second book, but more importantly for us it marks the end of this psalm. 'Blessed be the Lord' – gratitude be given to him who takes away our sins.

LET US PRAY: *Like the people in the gospel, Lord God, we praise you joyfully that your Son has come to bring forgiveness of sins. We acknowledge that through our selfishness we have contributed to the poverty and suffering in the world; of that sinfulness we now pray that we may be healed.*

Eighth Sunday in Ordinary Time

God's relation to his people is like that of a husband to his wife (Hosea 2:16-17, 21-22). Yet though he loves them dearly, they have been unfaithful; and so God plans to lure them back into the desert, confident that there the affection of courtship days will be renewed.

In the gospel (Mark 2:18-22) Jesus identifies himself as 'the bridegroom'. His presence means the fashioning of a new, everlasting covenant; it's a time for feasting not for fasting, a time for new wine and fresh skins! Fasting and other similar practices are a means to an end, not an end in themselves.

Paul (2 Corinthians 3:1-6) gives an exciting insight into the meaning of the covenant when he compares Christians to a letter, written by God with the Holy Spirit as the 'ink', by which Jesus Christ is revealed to others.

The responsorial psalm, an excerpt from Psalm 102, praises the love and compassion of our God.

Prayerful Ponderings

'My soul, give thanks to the Lord, all my being, bless his holy name. My soul, give thanks to the Lord and never forget all his blessings.'

A psalm of thanksgiving, like a psalm of praise, is usually obvious from the outset, because it begins with a call to thank/praise 'the Lord'. But whereas the call normally goes out to others, here it is addressed to the psalmist. The very core of the psalmist's 'being' is to be caught up in blessing the 'holy name' of God and, whatever else happens, is 'never [to] forget all his blessings'. A spirit of thanksgiving, a spirit of remembrance, as opposed to a spirit of forgetfulness, is the mark of a true follower of the Lord.

'It is he who forgives all your guilt, who heals every one of your ills, who redeems your life from the grave, who crowns you with love and compassion.'

This verse summarises the reasons why we must never forget: because God has so generously forgiven 'all [our] guilt', has brought healing to 'every one of [our] ills', has redeemed us by making us sharers in a life that lasts beyond 'the grave', has crowned our whole life and all that we are 'with [his] love and compassion'. The effects of the everlasting covenant brought into being by Jesus Christ are revolutionary: we are like a letter, written by the Father in the ink of the Holy Spirit, so that we may reveal to the world the characteristic traits of Jesus himself (see second reading).

'The Lord is compassion and love, slow to anger and rich in mercy.'
The first half of this verse forms the refrain of today's responsorial psalm and neatly sums up all of today's readings. In an attempt to express God's goodness, the psalmist resorts to repeating the description of himself that God gave to Moses on Mount Sinai (see Exodus 34:6). 'The Lord' is not simply compassionate and loving: he 'is compassion' itself, 'love' itself. All that we understand by those two words is to be found, without limit, in God. And so he is 'slow to anger and rich in mercy'.

'He does not treat us according to our sins nor repay us according to our faults. So far as the east is from the west so far does he remove our sins.'
In God's treatment of us, we catch a glimpse of what is meant by his 'amazing grace': he does not act in accordance with strict justice. In spite of our defiance and disloyalty, he is ready to cast 'our sins' and 'faults' away 'so far as the east is from the west'. They couldn't be cast further!

'As a father has compassion on his sons, the Lord has pity on those who fear him.'
The secret that lies behind God's dealings with us is the vastness of his fatherly love. Treating us 'as a father' treats his beloved 'sons', he takes account of our human frailty, and the moment that we show that 'fear' and awe, essential ingredients in every true act of sorrow, he 'has pity on [us]', restores us to his friendship.

LET US PRAY: *Heavenly Father, keep us ever mindful of the love and compassion that you show us, so that we never cease to rejoice in the covenant that you have made with us, the steadfast love with which you surround us and the forgiveness that you always offer to those who seek it.*

Ninth Sunday in Ordinary Time

Today's readings centre upon the Sabbath day. Just as the Jewish Sabbath had a spiritual meaning, as a sign of God's creative and redeeming work (Deuteronomy 5:12-15), so too does the Christian Sunday, as a celebration of the Easter mystery.

But even a precious law can be interpreted in a legalistic way. In the gospel (Mark 2:23-3:6) Jesus reacts against those who would turn the Sabbath into a day when the command to love one's neighbour can be forgotten in anxiety for the minutiae of the law.

The creator God who, through his Son Jesus, brought us from death to life, is the God who brings light to Paul in the midst of all the darkness of life's hardships and difficulties (2 Corinthians 4:6-11).

Psalm 80, which provides today's responsorial psalm, is an invitation to the seven-day festival of Tabernacles. During this great harvest festival, the people would dwell in shelters (or 'tabernacles') made of branches as though reliving the years of Israel's sojourn in the desert. The powerful sound of a ram's-horn trumpet, the *shophar*, would signal the new moon and the start of the month in which the feast was to be celebrated. Fifteen days later, it would signal the full moon which marked the first day of the feast itself.

Prayerful Ponderings

'Ring out your joy to God our strength.'
These words, which form the refrain of the responsorial psalm, are also the opening words of the psalm itself and set the tone for what follows. The people are invited to a festival, a gloriously happy occasion when they are to 'ring out [their] joy', as they recall how 'God is our strength'. Every time we worship the Lord together, it should be an occasion of joy. Vatican II spoke powerfully of Sunday, 'the original feast day' for Christians and the feast which gave rise to all the other festivals of the year. More recently Pope John Paul has spoken of 'the intense acclamations of joy which have always characterised Sunday in the liturgy of both East and West' (On Keeping Sunday Holy, 55).

'Raise a song and sound the timbrel, the sweet-sounding harp and the lute, blow the trumpet at the new moon, when the moon is full, on our feast.'
An assortment of musical instruments - 'the timbrel' (a kind of tambourine), 'the harp and the lute'- are to accompany the festive 'song'. Our liturgies may seem a good deal 'tamer' than the ones the psalmist was used to - though of course even today song and sometimes dance, vestments and altar vessels, signs of peace and occasional rounds of clapping, flowers and plants, all express the joy of celebration.

'For this is Israel's law, a command of the God of Jacob. He imposed it as a rule on Joseph, when he went out against the land of Egypt.'

There is reference to 'law', to 'a command of the God of Jacob', to 'a rule imposed' (by God). Yet how easily human beings can add to what God has decreed and hedge it about with all manner of restrictions so that instead of its being for our good, as God intended, it acts against our best interests. When pettifogging interpretations of the Sabbath law would condemn hungry disciples for picking ears of corn (harvesting on the holy day!) or Jesus himself for healing a man with a shrivelled hand (providing medical help outside danger of death on the holy day!), then Jesus is very angry. He knows that 'The Sabbath was made for man, not man for the Sabbath' (see today's gospel).

'A voice I did not know said to me: "I freed your shoulder from the burden; your hands were freed from the load. You called in distress and I saved you."'

The unknown 'voice' is that of God himself. It recalls his saving work, especially that of the Exodus, when he 'freed' his people from an arduous captivity and led them to their own land. It is summed up in two balancing statements: 'You called' ... 'I saved'. But of course consequences follow: the first, though not specifically mentioned at this point, is that God shall be honoured and worshipped: 'Remember the Sabbath day, and keep it holy' (Exodus 20:8).

'"Let there be no foreign god among you, no worship of an alien god. I am the Lord your God, who brought you from the land of Egypt."'

There is another consequence of the Exodus: there shall be 'no foreign god', 'no worship of an alien god'. However, 'foreign gods' come in many forms. It might be said that in our Lord's day the law itself had become a false god: it, or at any rate the regulations surrounding it, had been turned into a kind of idol, robbing people of the very freedom that God wanted them to have. In our own day, we are faced with the opposite extreme: for most people, Sunday has lost its special character, the rhythm of life has gone, Sundays have been turned into weekdays, the shopping mall has become the 'alien god'. The God-intended Sabbath rest has been forfeited, and we are the losers.

LET US PRAY: *Lord, God of the Exodus and God of Calvary, help us to recover the true meaning of the Sabbath. May every Sunday be an occasion for rejoicing and worshipping with Christian brothers and sisters; and may it be an occasion also for us to rest, to renew our strength and to rejoice in your creation which is 'good, very good'.*

Tenth Sunday in Ordinary Time

The first reading (Genesis 3:9-15) introduces the perennial struggle that takes place between 'the serpent' (the devil) and Adam and Eve (Mr and Mrs Everyman), but it also hints at One stronger than the serpent, the Messiah Son of God.

In the second reading (2 Corinthians 4:13-5:1) Paul sees us involved in a daily conflict, weighed down with bodily suffering and the prospect of death itself. But he also foresees 'a weight of eternal glory' and the prospect of an 'everlasting home'.

In the gospel (Mark 3:20-35), Jesus shows himself to be stronger than any devil and he assures us that, despite all difficulties, so long as we do 'the will of God' we belong to his family.

Psalm 129, today's responsorial psalm, is better known to many by the opening words of its Latin version *De profundis*. However, though linked with prayer for the dead, it is also one of the traditional 'penitential psalms', dealing with the predicament in which we find ourselves because of sin and with our need of God's grace.

Prayerful Ponderings

'Out of the depths I cry to you, O Lord, Lord, hear my voice!
O let your ears be attentive to the voice of my pleading.'
The immediate effect of sin, as the first reading suggests, is
separation. Sin separates us from each other, it separates us from
God, it separates us from the rest of creation. And so, because we
are sinners, we 'cry' to him 'out of the depths'. Sometimes the
struggles of life make us feel that there is a vast gulf between him
and us; we beg him to 'hear my voice', as though he might have
difficulty in picking up our far-away prayer, we plead with him 'let
your ears be attentive' so that they may catch the slightest sound of
our distant 'pleading'.

'If you, O Lord, should mark our guilt, Lord, who would survive?
But with you is found forgiveness: for this we revere you.'
We acknowledge that if the Lord were to 'mark our guilt', either in
the sense of being always on the watch to catch us out in sin, or in
the sense of holding sin unalterably against us, there would be no
escape and no hope for any of us. Indeed, if that were the case, then
the rhetorical question of the psalmist would be on the lips of
every one of us: 'Lord, who would survive?' But that is not the true
state of affairs; we believe that 'forgiveness' itself, and therefore
forgiveness without limit, 'is found' in him. In a spirit of awe and
wonder, 'we revere' him.

'My soul is waiting for the Lord, I count on his word. My soul is longing for the Lord more than watchman for daybreak.' Our trust in him is unshakeable. We wait for him and know that our 'waiting' can never be in vain, for 'his word' is reliable, it can always be counted upon. That he will come is as sure as is 'daybreak' for the 'watchman' who waits to be relieved from his post, or, as we might say, that he will come is as sure as night follows day. It is often said that 'God helps those who help themselves'; this psalm suggests that God helps even those who are unable to help themselves – apart from waiting trustfully 'for the Lord'.

'Because with the Lord there is mercy and fullness of redemption, Israel indeed he will redeem from all its iniquity.' Sin is often ridiculed as an archaic idea, and yet we live in a century where sin has spawned so many terrible evils; we need only think of Auschwitz, of Tiananmen Square, of world-wide use of torture, of the atomic bomb and its successors, of the damage done by human greed to the ozone layer and the trees of rain forests. It can seem a hopeless situation, and yet because 'there is mercy and fullness of redemption' with our God, we pray confidently for a redemption that will benefit not merely ourselves but the whole of humanity and 'redeem' it from 'all its iniquity'.

LET US PRAY: *Lord, out of the depths of our own sins and out of the depths of the sins of the whole world, we wait for you; we count upon you and your unfailing word; we beg that through our Saviour Jesus the devil's wiles will finally be defeated and all humanity may rejoice in your salvation.*

Eleventh Sunday in Ordinary Time

Today's readings breathe a spirit of confidence. The prophet Ezekiel (17:22-24) promises that just as a majestic cedar grows from a tender shoot, so God will enable a new people to arise from the tiny remnant of Israel.

By means of parables (Mark 4:26-34) Jesus teaches us that as the seed that is sown achieves its purpose in hidden fashion, so God, despite his apparent inactivity, is always secretly at work for the success of the kingdom; that, as the tiny mustard seed becomes a huge bush, so despite lowly beginnings the growth and spread of the kingdom are assured.

Paul too (2 Corinthians 5:6-10) speaks of the confidence Christians enjoy as sharers in the life of Christ. Though the fruit in all its richness is yet to come, 'we are full of confidence' and 'intent on pleasing him'.

The responsorial psalm (Psalm 91) is a song of gratitude to God for his goodness, in particular for the way he ensures that the just 'flourish like the palm tree and ... a Lebanon cedar'.

Prayerful Ponderings

'It is good to give thanks to the Lord, to make music to your name, O Most High ...'
The first phrase, which also serves as the refrain for the responsorial psalm, sums up the whole of Psalm 91: quite simply, giving 'thanks to the Lord' is 'good'; it makes 'music to [his] name'. The Lord values it, as he values the work of creation – which he also saw to be good (Genesis 1:4,10,12,18,21,25,31) – not only because it gives God what is his due; but also because it enables us to fulfil a basic duty and thereby be saved from selfish ingratitude. In the gospel Jesus is revealed as a grateful man, deeply conscious that he has received everything from the Father and always ready to raise his voice in thanksgiving, even on the eve of his passion and death; it would be strange indeed to call ourselves his followers if we did not emulate his spirit of gratitude and praise.

'... to proclaim your love in the morning and your truth in the watches of the night.'
The reasons for gratitude, the psalmist suggests, are reducible to two: on the one hand, there is the Lord's covenant 'love', his unswerving devotion to us; and on the other his 'truth' or reliability – the word for truth, 'emet, comes from the same root as 'Amen'; it speaks of what is solid and dependable. Reflection on these characteristics of the Lord leads us to praise and thank him 'morning' and 'night': we are forever indebted to him.

'The just will flourish like the palm-tree and grow like a Lebanon cedar.'

In today's second reading, Paul states that 'each of us will get what he deserves'. The psalm makes the same point. The verses immediately preceding this one (they do not appear in today's responsorial psalm) declare that it is only 'the fool' that fails to appreciate all that the Lord has done and they go on to outline the fate of the wicked. However, 'the just' can look forward to flourishing like impressive trees of the forest – like 'the [stately] palm-tree' which stands erect and yet is able to bend, without breaking, before a gale; and like 'a Lebanon cedar', renowned for its size and strength and endurance.

'Planted in the house of the Lord, they will flourish in the courts of our God, still bearing fruit when they are old, still full of sap, still green, to proclaim that the Lord is just. In him, my rock, there is no wrong.'

Again we are reminded that the just are kept close to the Lord ('planted in [his] house', flourishing in his 'courts') and so they prosper. Among elderly people, it's wonderful to meet those who despite age are spiritually 'still bearing fruit when they are old, still full of sap, still green'. By the very way they live their lives, they 'proclaim' and glorify God. Young and old alike are invited to acknowledge that the Lord is our 'rock' and in him 'there is no wrong': he can be depended upon with absolute confidence.

LET US PRAY: *It is indeed good to give thanks to you, Lord our God; grant us, then, grateful, trusting hearts, that all our life through it may be our delight to praise you, to thank you and to place our trust in you.*

Twelfth Sunday in Ordinary Time

In the first reading (Job 3:1, 8-11) the Lord addresses Job, declaring that only he, the Lord, has power to control the tempestuous seas.

In the gospel (Mark 4:35-41) Jesus calms a storm on the Lake of Galilee; friends are left wondering: 'Who can this be? Even the wind and the sea obey him.'

Psalm 106 might be described as a portmanteau song of thanksgiving because its centrepiece is made up of four sections, each detailing a specific danger from which God has set people free and calling upon those rescued to give thanks. Not surprisingly, the section which has been chosen as today's responsorial psalm concerns the rescue of troubled seafarers, a section which seems to have been the inspiration for the sailors' hymn 'Eternal Father ,strong to save'.

The second reading (2 Corinthians 5:14-17) also pays tribute to the amazing power of our God, who in love has conquered all our enemies and made of us 'a new creation'.

Prayerful Ponderings

'O give thanks to the Lord, for his love endures for ever.'
This is the introduction to a psalm which bids us 'give thanks to the Lord' because of 'his (faithful) love' which 'endures for ever'. It is a love which has been manifested in his saving interventions in response to the cries of those in distress.

'Some sailed to the sea in ships to trade on the mighty waters. These men have seen the Lord's deeds, the wonders he does in the deep. For he spoke; he summoned the gale, tossing the waves of the sea up to heaven and back into the deep; their soul melted away in their distress.'
Each of the four central sections of the psalm is constructed in much the same way. It begins with an account of adversity – here it is a fearful storm at sea. The 'men' affected were a group of merchants who had learned how 'to trade on the mighty waters'. No doubt on many occasions they had caught a glimpse of 'the Lord's deeds' as they contended with the devastating power of an angry sea. This time, however, a fiercer 'gale' than ever had blown up. They felt themselves being hoisted 'up to heaven' and then plunged 'back into the deep'; their courage simply 'melted away'. A verse, not included in today's responsorial psalm, adds that they 'reeled like drunken men' – just to read about them makes one feel a little sea-sick!

'Then they cried to the Lord in their need and he rescued them from their distress. He stilled the storm to a whisper: all the waves of the sea were hushed.'

After the description of the storm-tossed sea and its effect on the hapless sailors, there comes a second feature common to each section of the psalm - the plea for help: 'they cried to the Lord in their need'. Then comes the third common feature – the story of deliverance: 'he rescued them from their distress'. 'The waves', which a short time before had been so threatening to the seafarers ,were now 'hushed'. In today's gospel it was Jesus' power to still the storm so that 'all was calm again' that had the disciples wondering about his identity – did they perhaps have this psalm in mind? Only God had power over the sea (see first reading).

'They rejoiced because of the calm and he led them to the haven they desired. Let them thank the Lord for his love, the wonders he does for men.'

Not only did the Lord reduce 'the storm to a whisper', he also brought the seafarers safely 'to the haven they desired'. And so to the fourth and final common feature of the various sections of this psalm: a call to praise and 'thank the Lord for his love'. Many commentators see the four types of adversity/deliverance as simply four different ways of describing the one great reality: the saving work of God, what the psalm calls 'the wonders he does for men [and women]'. We see those wonders supremely in the life of Jesus - in his feeding the hungry in the wilderness, in his calming the storm at sea, in his freeing people from sin and, above all, in his death and resurrection. He is our great redeemer, rescuing us from all that threatens our well-being and making it possible for us to reach our ultimate 'haven'.

LET US PRAY: *Confident of your unchanging love and of your readiness to respond to all who cry to you for help, we beg you, Saviour Lord, to be with us amid the storms of this life so that we may come safely through adversity and one day reach our heavenly home.*

Thirteenth Sunday in Ordinary Time

Since the world began men and women have struggled with the problem of making sense of death. In the book of Wisdom (1:13-15; 2:23-24), it is stated clearly that 'virtue is undying', life does not end with death.

It is above all in the ministry, death and resurrection of Jesus that the gift of everlasting life is revealed. His miracles, such as those recounted in today's gospel (Mark 5:21-43), are signs that he has broken decisively the death-dealing power of the devil.

Paul teaches us (2 Corinthians 8:7, 9, 13-15) that Jesus 'became poor... to make (us) rich', rich above all by our sharing in his eternal life. That gift should lead us to follow his example by giving of our riches to those who are poor.

Today's responsorial psalm is appropriately made up of verses from Psalm 29, which is itself a thanksgiving song for recovery from a life-threatening sickness.

Prayerful Ponderings

'I will praise you, Lord, you have rescued me and have not let my enemies rejoice over me.'
From the outset – in words which form the refrain for the responsorial psalm – the purpose of the psalmist is clear: it is to 'praise' or, perhaps better, to extol the 'Lord' who has 'rescued me'. And so 'my enemies', who would have taken pleasure in my misfortune, now have nothing to rejoice over! The expression of such sentiments is a reminder that the psalmists live in the real world, where, alas, one person's calamity does sometimes afford pleasure to another, but it is also a clear indication that, when they speak to God in prayer, the psalmists feel no need to sanitise their words; they are ready to 'tell it as it is'.

'O Lord, you have raised my soul from the dead, restored me to life from those who sink into the grave.'
And this is what the psalmist has been rescued from – death, the company of 'the dead'. The Hebrew expression for 'raised' might be used of drawing a bucket up from a well, and so conveys a vivid picture: God hauling up the psalmist from the deep well of death. So it is that 'you have ... restored me to life', enabling me to escape the fate of those who lie in 'the grave'.

'Sing psalms to the Lord, you who love him, give thanks to his holy name.'

Having described his own narrow escape from death, the psalmist feels the need to have others – at any rate, those 'who love' the Lord – to join him, so that together they may 'sing psalms to the Lord' and 'give thanks to his holy name'. At every Mass we are called not only as individuals but also as community to 'sing [or at any rate to pray] psalms' and 'give thanks', especially for the gift of everlasting life; since we have been saved as members of a community, thanksgiving is our communal responsibility.

'His anger lasts but a moment; his favour through life. At night there are tears, but joy comes with dawn.'
God's 'anger' is the cause of the trouble, the psalmist seems to say, yet, he adds, that anger is only momentary. 'His favour', on the other hand, his kindliness, accompanies us all 'through life'; 'tears' are like overnight guests, they don't stay long, and 'with the dawn' comes another day and with it 'joy' to replace sorrow. We may be unable to share the psalmist's view about the connection between sickness and God's anger, but we too know that the keenest pain, like that of a woman in labour, can prepare the way for a joy that far outstrips the suffering (John 16:20–22); indeed, we believe that in heaven 'a weight of glory' awaits us 'which is out of all proportion' to the troubles and afflictions of life.

'The Lord listened and had pity. The Lord came to my help. For me you have changed my mourning into dancing, O Lord my God, I will thank you for ever.'
The psalmist ends in much the same way as he began, by proclaiming how 'The Lord listened' to him, heard his prayer, showed him 'pity'. He celebrates the way 'the Lord came to my

help' by use of another striking image: you have 'changed' the drab heaviness of 'mourning' into the joyful gladness of 'dancing'. Finally, the psalmist cries out that he 'will thank [God] for ever'; probably he means no more than that so long as life lasts, he will be grateful to God. Yet his words, taken literally, are an exact expression of our own Christian hope: that neither tears, nor pain, nor even death itself, will have the last word, and that beyond death it will be our glory to thank God for ever.

LET US PRAY: *Loving Father, thanks to the resurrection of your Son, our Lord Jesus Christ, we believe that death, our last great enemy, will not rejoice over us; and despite the pain and suffering that we may experience at the end of life on this earth, we have confidence that you will change our mourning into dancing and that we shall thank you for ever.*

Fourteenth Sunday in Ordinary Time

Despite the painfulness of opposition, the prophet Ezekiel, supported by the Lord, will not be deterred from continuing his task (Ezekiel 2:2-5).

Jesus, too, had to cope with opposition even from his own townspeople and it obviously hurt him: 'He was amazed at their lack of faith' (Mark 6:1-6).

Paul faced not only opposition from without, but also weakness from within ('a thorn in the flesh'), but continued his work in the conviction that 'it is when I am weak that I am strong' (2 Corinthians 12:7-10).

The psalmist - today's responsorial psalm is the whole of Psalm 122 - also knows what it means to meet with 'contempt' and 'disdain'.

Prayerful Ponderings

'To you have I lifted up my eyes, you who dwell in the heavens.'
These opening words set the theme for a psalm which is at once a song of petition and a song of confidence. It's the song of one whose 'eyes' are raised to 'the heavens' and, more precisely, to him who dwells there. It's the song of one who faces the scorn and arrogance of the rich. It's the song of one of the *anawim*, those 'people humble and lowly' (Zephaniah 3:12), who turn trustingly to the Lord, the champion of the poor and distressed. Psalm 122 is the fourth of the fifteen 'songs of ascent', which were used by pilgrims on their way up to Jerusalem for the great feasts. Their eyes scanned the heights, eager for the first glimpse of the Holy City, but the eyes of their hearts must often have soared higher still – towards heaven, towards the Lord.

'My eyes, like the eyes of slaves on the hand of their lords. Like the eyes of a servant on the hand of his mistress, so our eyes are on the Lord our God till he show us his mercy.'
The song of an individual psalmist becomes the song of his companions, too – note how 'my eyes' become 'our eyes'; in their expectant waiting on 'the Lord', they are like a group of 'slaves' whose 'eyes' are set hopefully on 'their lords', alert for a movement of 'the hand' or some other similar sign, which will show that they

are to receive the favour they long for. Or again, the pilgrims are like a 'servant' girl who is all 'eyes' on her mistress, confident that the lady will not disappoint her. If slaves and servants can rely upon their superior for help, how much more can we who have heard the glorious assurance of St Paul: 'you are no longer a slave but a child' (Galatians 4:7). And so when, with the refrain of today's responsorial psalm, we say over and over again that 'Our eyes are on the Lord till he show us his mercy', we do so with boundless trust, for we know that he to whom we look is our Abba (dear Father), always ready to listen to his sons and daughters.

'Have mercy on us, Lord, have mercy. We are filled with contempt. Indeed all too full is our soul with the scorn of the rich, with proud man's disdain.'
The petition of the pilgrims is simple enough: that the Lord will 'have mercy on [them]', will show them his favour. We are not told the exact nature of their request, beyond the fact that in place of the 'contempt', 'scorn' and 'disdain' they experience at the hands of 'the rich' and 'proud', they pray that they may enjoy the graciousness of the Lord himself. It is doubtless the kind of prayer that was prayed by Ezekiel, by Paul and even by Jesus himself when they had to contend with opposition and insults (see today's readings).

LET US PRAY: *Faithful Lord, when we have to face opposition or difficulties from whatever quarter, may we have the wisdom to raise our eyes confidently towards you so that we may experience the comfort of your gracious support.*

Fifteenth Sunday in Ordinary Time

In the eighth century BC, Amos, the southerner, had the unenviable task of prophesying in Bethel, the royal sanctuary of the North. Amaziah, priest of the sanctuary, bids him return home, but Amos, knowing that God himself bade him speak, will not be deterred (Amos 7:12-15).

In the gospel (Mark 6:7-13) Jesus sends out the Twelve to announce the good news of the kingdom. They are to travel light, to preach and heal and cast out devils, and not to be surprised if they meet with opposition.

The letter to the Ephesians begins with a passage (1:3-14) which outlines the wonderful plan of God by which we were chosen, had our sins forgiven, and have been made into 'adopted sons' (and daughters).

The lines from Psalm 84 which make up the responsorial psalm might serve as a reflection on today's second reading, for they speak with confidence of the plans that the Lord has worked out for us, plans which were hinted at in the proclamation of the prophets (first reading) and illuminated by the preaching of Christ and his apostles (gospel).

Prayerful Ponderings

'Let us see, O Lord, your mercy and give us your saving help.' This psalm was written after the Israelites returned from exile: it begins with a look back to those heady days when God 'favoured his land and revived the fortunes' of his people. But despite that wonderful saving intervention, the answer to all their prayers, things didn't always turn out as they had hoped: they still had to face disappointments and frustrations. And so they beg him once again to 'let [them] see' his unfailing love and 'saving help'. We too pray in similar vein: there is a sense in which we have been saved, and yet there is also a sense in which we constantly plead that we may be saved. Life has its ups and downs, and in the difficult times it is especially the thought of all that the Lord has done in the past that gives us confidence to seek his help once more.

'I will hear what the Lord God has to say, a voice that speaks of peace, peace for his people.'
It appears that in the course of the liturgy, which was the original setting for the psalm, the voice of an individual (notice the 'I') was suddenly heard – it was perhaps that of a prophet, or a priest, or some other temple minister. He reminds fellow-worshippers that he has heard – and perhaps it is implied that they too have heard, or at any rate should have heard – 'what the Lord God has to say'. From childhood days they have been taught that his voice is 'a

voice that [always] speaks of peace', for he is concerned with all that is in their best interests. There are times when we all need to be reminded of that solid truth: that God longs, even more than we do ourselves, for our happiness and peace. At the same time, the words of the anonymous speaker serve as a warning, especially in view of the rejection of Amos (first reading) and the promised rejection of the apostles (gospel): even when God does speak we can be deaf to his voice because we do not recognise him in his messenger.

'His help is near for those who fear him and his glory will dwell in our land.'
The speaker draws the conclusion that God's 'help is near', at any rate for those who hold him in reverential 'fear', and he goes on to promise that God's 'glory will [once more] dwell in our land'. Yet even he could never have imagined that that glory would one day be present in the person of a man who trod this earth, living not simply with us but as one of us, a man in whom 'the fullness of God was pleased to dwell' (Colossians 1:19). An antiphon from the Prayer of the Church for Christmas Eve comes to mind: 'Know today that the Lord will come; in the morning you will see his glory'. In the child in the manger we gain an insight into the passionate love that God has for us and 'our land', this crazy, mixed-up little planet on which we dwell. Pope John Paul II has written: 'By his Incarnation, [Jesus] united himself in some sense with every person.' His help is indeed far nearer than we could have imagined possible, and his glory dwells within us.

'Mercy and faithfulness have met; justice and peace have embraced. Faithfulness shall spring from the earth and justice look down from heaven.'

In Jesus Christ the reconciliation of heaven and earth is achieved; in his person a combination of the divine attributes is 'embraced' in perfect harmony: 'mercy' (steadfast love) and 'faithfulness', 'justice' (righteousness) and 'peace'. In spite of everything, God loves this 'earth' of ours; nor does he simply 'look down from heaven' upon it, he sends his Son to live on it and to die for all who dwell there.

'The Lord will make us prosper and our earth shall yield its fruit. Justice shall march before him and peace shall follow his steps.'

The opening chapter of the letter to the Ephesians (second reading) is a wonderful summary of how 'the Lord' has made 'us prosper' and how 'our earth' has yielded 'fruit' beyond our wildest expectations: through his Son, born of a woman of this earth, we have been blessed with all the spiritual blessings of heaven, we have become adopted sons and daughters, we have gained our freedom by forgiveness of our sins. In almost every gospel passage Our Lord is presented as dispensing a largesse of blessings wherever he goes: divine 'justice' (saving mercy) marches forth in his person and 'peace' follows in 'his [foot]steps'.

LET US PRAY: *Lord our God, make us alert to hear your voice, especially when you speak to us in unanticipated ways and through unexpected people, and in all the difficulties of life may we find encouragement in the blessings already showered upon us through your dear Son, Jesus Christ.*

Sixteenth Sunday in Ordinary Time

The shepherding care of God is a central theme of today's readings. In the first (Jreremiah 23:1-6), Jeremiah castigates the rulers of Judah, describing them as bad shepherds, and promising that God will raise up other shepherds, including a descendant of David who will prove to be a good shepherd to his people.

In the gospel (Mark 6:30-34) that Davidic descendant, full of concern for the 'large crowd' who are 'like sheep without a shepherd', offers them nourishment both for their minds and hearts (his teaching) and for their bodies (food).

Predictably, the responsorial psalm is the whole of Psalm 22, the famous song of confidence and trust in the good shepherd.

The second reading (Ephesians 2:13-18) tells how Jesus achieved the reconciliation of humankind with God by his death on the cross - the good shepherd lays down his life for his sheep.

Prayerful Ponderings

'The Lord is my shepherd; there is nothing I shall want.'
These opening words, which also form the refrain of today's responsorial psalm, set the scene for all that follows, but they are not without a challenge for those who pray them. In the ancient Near East kings were often known as shepherds because their task was to protect their people, meet their needs, preserve the peace; in today's first reading the kings are described as evil shepherds precisely because they failed in these duties. However, 'The Lord is my [good] shepherd' because he is all that they were not: he is my protector, my source of peace, my benefactor; he is totally dedicated to me and all that concerns me. And so I am led to pray - and here comes the challenge - 'there is nothing I shall want'. It takes courage to repeat, and really mean, these words: that ultimately God alone is all that I want, he alone fulfils all my deepest needs; I want him no matter what the cost.

'Fresh and green are the pastures where he gives me repose. Near restful waters he leads me, to revive my drooping spirit. He guides me along the right path; he is true to his name.'
With a series of simple vignettes the psalm speaks of the way the Lord shows his pastoral concern - by providing me with 'green pastures', with 'repose' and rest, and, in difficult times, by reviving my 'drooping spirit'. 'He guides me along the right path', teaches

me the way I should go. And all this because 'he is true to his name', which in this context might be reworded 'because he is faithful to his covenant of friendship with me'.

'If I should walk in the valley of darkness no evil would I fear. You are there with your crook and your staff; with these you give me comfort. You have prepared a banquet for me in the sight of my foes. My head you have anointed with oil; my cup is overflowing.'
To have the Lord as shepherd is no guarantee of a trouble-free existence. On the contrary, I am as likely as anyone else to face 'the valley of darkness' in one shape or another; but what makes the difference is the comfort brought me by the presence of my shepherd. In this middle section of the psalm the shepherd is not spoken of as 'he' but rather as 'you'. It's as though, particularly in times of trouble, his presence is often most keenly felt; he is no longer simply someone I speak about (an object almost) but someone who is actually with me (a personal presence). He is armed with 'crook and staff', to overcome my enemies – and no doubt to urge me on when I tend to lag behind. And so 'fear' will not have the last word.

At this point there is a change of image: the good shepherd becomes the generous host; the one who offered me protection, now prepares 'a banquet for me'; there is 'oil' for my head, and an overflowing 'cup' to delight my palate. These signs of hospitality also put me in mind of the sacraments in which the Lord sees to my deepest spiritual needs through such everyday objects as bread and wine, water and oil.

'Surely goodness and kindness shall follow me all the days of my life. In the Lord's own house shall I dwell for ever.' All the Lord's dealings give me deep confidence that his 'goodness and kindness' – the characteristics of the covenant relationship between us – will never fail; indeed, they will 'follow me all the days of my life'. And even when those days are completed, I confidently trust that, through his merciful goodness, I shall have a place 'in the Lord's own house' and that there 'I [shall] dwell for ever'.

LET US PRAY: *Jesus, our good shepherd, take care of the Church, your 'little flock'; may it always be blessed with good and zealous pastors who will lead it faithfully in your ways.*

Seventeenth Sunday
in Ordinary Time

In the first reading (2 Kings 4:42-44) we hear how Elisha the prophet miraculously feeds 'a hundred men' with twenty barley loaves.

The gospel (John 6:1-15) records that, when the apostles were faced with the 'impossible' task of feeding a great crowd of five thousand people, Jesus himself intervened, providing food for all from five barley loaves and a couple of fish.

The responsorial psalm, which consists of a few verses from Psalm 144, emphasises God's provision of food for his hungry creatures.

The second reading (Ephesians 4:1-6) calls to mind that God has met our deepest spiritual needs by making us his children and by uniting us all in one Body, built up by one baptism and sustained with one faith and one hope.

Prayerful Ponderings

'All your creatures shall thank you, O Lord, and your friends shall repeat their blessing. They shall speak of the glory of your reign and declare your might, O God.'

Psalm 144 is an outpouring of praise to a God whose 'greatness cannot be measured', a God of 'splendour and majesty', a God of 'abundant goodness', a God 'of compassion' and 'abounding in love' (see the earlier verses of this psalm). It is hardly surprising then that 'all your creatures' should feel the need to 'thank you, O Lord', to 'speak of the glory' of your rule, and to 'declare your might'. However, while other creatures give thanks unconsciously, simply by what they are – the birds by their graceful flight and enchanting song, the flowers by their incredible beauty, the wild animals by their mighty strength, and so on – it is only human beings that can offer personal thanks; it is only we who can enter into personal friendship with God. And so it is supremely we 'your friends' who consciously and willingly 'repeat [the] blessing', the thanksgiving, of the rest of creation.

'The eyes of all creatures look to you and you give them their food in due time. You open wide your hand, grant the desires of all who live.'

Over the centuries these verses have been used as a grace before meals in many a monastery, convent and seminary. They are an acknowledgement that our 'food' is always a gift from God, and no less 'miraculous' because it is due not directly to divine intervention (see today's readings) but, in part at least, to 'work of human hands'. It is also an acknowledgement that our God is an open-handed God, eager to meet 'the desires of all'. Two thoughts come to mind: the first, that without our co-operation many of our fellow men and women will look in vain for the food they need – God depends upon us to feed the hungry of the world; and second, that to sit down to our meals without a prayer of blessing means, as Bishop Butler used to say, that we are behaving as something less than human - something like animals at feeding time in a zoo!

'The Lord is just in all his ways and loving in all his deeds. He is close to all who call him, who call on him from their hearts.' All the Lord's dealings with us are characterised by justice and love; and we, in all our ways, ought to be 'just' and 'loving', too. There is immense comfort in the conviction that 'he is close', close not simply in the sense of able to hear but rather with the closeness of friendship to 'all who call on him'. According to the visionaries of Medjugorje, Our Lady constantly urged the children to 'pray from the heart'; long before, the psalmist had recognised the need for prayer from the heart from the friends of the Lord.

LET US PRAY: *Mighty God, forgive us for the times we have taken your countless gifts for granted; make us truly grateful, not least for the 'daily bread' - the bread of our meals and the bread of the Eucharist - which you provide.*

Eighteenth Sunday
in Ordinary Time

In response to their complaining about inadequacy of food during their desert wanderings, God provides the people of Israel with manna, 'bread from the heavens', which they will receive a day at a time (Exodus 16:2-4, 12-15). It will be both a sign of God's care and a challenge to their trust in him.

In the gospel (John 6:24-35), taken today and for the next three Sundays from St John's Gospel, Jesus tells the people that the Father provides the real bread from heaven - himself. Whoever comes to him will never hunger.

Psalm 77 is a lengthy historical psalm; the handful of verses which make up today's responsorial psalm describe God's gifts to his people of bread and of land.

The second reading (Ephesians 4:17, 20-24) calls for 'a spiritual revolution', a new way of living which will reflect the source of Christian living, Jesus Christ. He is the food on which we are to be nourished.

Prayerful Ponderings

'The things we have heard and understood, the things our fathers have told us, we will tell to the next generation: the glories of the Lord and his might.'

The psalm is the speech or sermon of an individual, perhaps one of the temple priests. The preacher no doubt hopes that by presenting his message in the form of a hymn, a psalm, it will be easier for the people, most of whom are illiterate, to remember it. Its purpose is clear: it is to instruct the people. Just as they 'heard' from 'our fathers', those who went before them, the good news of the wonderful deeds of God on behalf of Israel ('the glories of the Lord and his might' is the way the preacher describes them), so they in their turn have the God-given duty of passing on that same good news to the men and women of 'the next generation'.

The psalm testifies to the crucial role that tradition played in biblical religion: the good news had to be preserved and passed down from generation to generation. And of course the same is true of Christianity, too: Vatican II states that 'The Church, in its teaching, life, and worship, perpetuates and hands on to all generations all that it is itself and all that it believes' (Constitution on Divine Revelation, 8). This is an appropriate occasion for us to give thanks for all that has come down to us through the Church, and in particular, on this Sunday, for the Holy Eucharist, the Bread of Life.

'He commanded the clouds above and opened the gates of heaven. He rained down manna for their food, and gave them bread from heaven. Mere men ate the bread of angels. He sent them abundance of food.'

The people of Israel must never forget the way God took care of them, especially when, under Moses' leadership, they trekked through the desert on their way to the Promised Land. In their hunger they cried out in complaint and God responded in unexpected fashion. The psalm envisages him giving the word of command to 'the clouds above' so that they open up and down pours 'manna' (see first reading). As today's gospel shows, people spoke of this 'abundance of food' as 'bread from heaven' and as 'the bread of angels'; indeed they suggest that Jesus prove that he is greater than Moses by working a miracle greater than that of the manna. His reply is first to point out that it wasn't Moses but God himself who provided that 'bread from heaven', and secondly, even more importantly, that that gift is surpassed by the gift that God now gives – the true bread from heaven, his only Son Jesus Christ!

'He brought them to his holy land, to the mountain which his right hand had won.'

The psalmist acknowledges that it was God who 'brought them' safely to their journey's end – to the 'holy land' and 'to the mountain' (presumably Mount Zion on which the Temple stood). Today we hear Jesus speaking of a bread from heaven which 'gives life to the whole world'; he is to be the food which will nourish us on our way to the 'holy land' of heaven, the 'mountain' height which he won for us not by the strength of 'his right hand' but by the lowly laying down of his life on our behalf.

LET US PRAY: *Faithful God, may we who are nourished on our pilgrimage journey by the true Bread of Life, the food of angels, be constantly renewed in the likeness of Jesus the Lord.*

Nineteenth Sunday
in Ordinary Time

The prophet Elijah, fleeing for his life from pagan queen Jezebel, arrives in the wilderness. He is convinced that he is a failure, but an angel comforts him, providing food for a long journey which will bring him to 'the mountain of God' (1 Kings 19:4-9).

In the gospel (John 6:41-51), when his hearers are murmuring against him, Jesus is all the more insistent that he is the true bread from heaven, bread that will enable us to 'live for ever'.

It is hardly surprising that we, who are 'children of [God] that he loves', should strive to live in accordance with our Christian dignity, especially in our dealings with others (Ephesians 4:30-5:2).

On this and on each of the following two Sundays, when the gospel passage is from our Lord's discourse on the Bread of Life (chapter 6 of St John's Gospel), the responsorial psalm is taken from the thanksgiving song Psalm 33, with the refrain 'Taste and see that the Lord is good'.

Prayerful Ponderings

'I will bless the Lord at all times, his praise always on my lips; in the Lord my soul shall make its boast. The humble shall hear and be glad.'

The psalmist is deeply committed to the Lord: prayers of praise and thanksgiving are 'always on my lips'. Furthermore, his intention is that it shall always be so: 'I will [in the future] bless' him 'at all times'; indeed, he is my soul's 'boast'. This confession will be a source of joy to all who are truly 'humble' of heart: they will 'hear and be glad'.

'Glorify the Lord with me. Together let us praise his name. I sought the Lord and he answered me; from all my terrors he set me free.'

This song is not only a psalm of thanksgiving, it is also a psalm of instruction. And so the psalmist urges others to follow his example and join in glorifying 'the Lord with me'; 'together', he cries, 'let us praise his name'. He can't resist the opportunity to recall how God set him free 'from all my terrors'. As we pray the psalm today we ought to be eager to respond to the psalmist's invitation: through Jesus, we are liberated from all our fears, we are set free, we are fed on the bread from heaven; we of all people ought to bless, and thank, and exalt the name of our God – and encourage others to do likewise, above all by the way we lead our lives (see second reading).

'Look towards him and be radiant; let your faces not be abashed. This poor man called; the Lord heard him and rescued him from all his distress. The angel of the Lord is encamped around those who revere him, to rescue them.'

'Be radiant', the psalmist urges us. The phrase is fascinating because in Isaiah 60 Jerusalem is pictured as a mother awaiting the return from exile of sons and daughters whom she had once thought that she would never see again; at their appearance her face is 'radiant' (the same word, *nhr*, as in the psalm). To 'look towards the Lord' in prayer is to be filled with joy, is to be free of shame. Once again the psalmist feels impelled to bear witness to his personal experience of being 'rescued... from all his distress'. The final words remind us of today's first reading, where God sends an angel to strengthen the disconsolate Elijah with food and drink. God's love for his people and power to save them have not lessened since the days of Elijah - or of the psalmist.

'Taste and see that the Lord is good. He is happy who seeks refuge in him.'

It may seem strange to speak of tasting the Lord, but is it not the psalmist's way of saying that if we pray, then we shall find out from personal experience, we shall come to know in our hearts, that 'the Lord is good'? And if that is true of prayer, it is in a unique sense true of the Eucharist in which we receive Jesus himself as 'the living bread come down from heaven'. There is happiness for anyone 'who seeks refuge in him', but again a unique happiness for those who receive him in Holy Communion.

LET US PRAY: *Lord Almighty, you have created all things for the sake of your name and have given them food and drink to enjoy, so that they may give thanks to you; but to us you have granted spiritual food and drink and eternal life through Jesus, your servant. (Taken from the Didache, a church order of the late first or early second century)*

Twentieth Sunday in Ordinary Time

God sent Lady Wisdom, who under the form of a banquet presents the food of understanding to those who are uninformed (Proverbs 9:1-6). 'Come', she says, 'eat my bread, drink the wine I have prepared!'

God sent his Son who under the form of bread and wine presents us with the banquet of his Body and Blood (John 6:51-58). 'Anyone', he says, 'who does eat my flesh and drink my blood has eternal life.'

The letter to the Ephesians urges us to be 'careful about the lives you lead', avoiding drunkenness but being intoxicated with the Spirit who fills our hearts (Ephesians 5:15-20).

Verses from Psalm 33 - most of them different from the ones which appeared last Sunday - make up today's responsorial psalm. The refrain remains: 'Taste and see that the Lord is good.'

Prayerful Ponderings

'I will bless the Lord at all times, his praise always on my lips; in the Lord my soul shall make its boast. The humble shall hear and be glad.'
The responsorial psalm begins on the same note as it did last week: the psalmist is confident that 'the humble' person will 'be glad' when he or she hears him proclaim that he blesses and praises God 'at all times' and intends 'always' to do so. However, this time the psalmist's words are reinforced by today's second reading which urges us 'to sing the words … of the psalms … when you are together, and go on singing … to the Lord in your hearts, so that always and everywhere you are giving thanks to God'.

'Revere the Lord, you his saints. They lack nothing, those who revere him. Strong lions suffer want and go hungry but those who seek the Lord lack no blessing.'
The psalmist wishes to offer instruction to all who will listen to him. 'Strong lions', he says, may 'go hungry' but 'his saints' (those who are his people), 'those who seek the Lord' – they 'lack no blessing'. It needs little ingenuity to see the relevance of his words for today: we can so easily be envious of the 'strong lions' in society, those who have power, wealth and influence. They seem to have everything and yet so often experience a terrible emptiness in their lives. On the other hand, many of those who seem to have nothing

are unbelievably rich in God's blessings; they might be described in the words of St Paul – 'as [apparently] having nothing, and yet [in fact] possessing everything' (2 Corinthians 6:10).

'Come, children, and hear me that I may teach you the fear of the Lord. Who is he who longs for life and many days, to enjoy his prosperity?'

The voice of instruction is clearly heard in these lines: the psalmist expressly sets out to 'teach' and he addresses his hearers as 'children' or, as we might say, pupils. What he wishes to teach them is how to 'fear … the Lord', how to show him the reverence that is his due, how to do his will. Teacher-like, he raises a question, well knowing what the answer will be! 'Who wants a long and prosperous life?' Of course, everyone does, but not even the psalmist could offer what Jesus offers in today's gospel – the promise of eternal life; not only life without end but also life in its fullness.

'Then keep your tongue from evil and your lips from speaking deceit. Turn aside from evil and do good; seek and strive after peace.'

The proof that we genuinely 'fear the Lord' is the way we lead our lives. The psalmist speaks of the need to watch our 'tongue' which, as St James powerfully reminds us, can so easily slip into wicked ways (James 3). In general terms, we are to avoid 'evil and do good', we are to 'seek and strive after [what makes for] peace'. In other words, our faith has ethical implications. That is why today's second reading points out that though we may live in 'a wicked age', yet as baptised Christians we must be 'very careful about the sort of lives [we] lead' and seek 'the will of the Lord'.

LET US PRAY: *Lord, in the bread and wine of the Holy Eucharist we taste and see your goodness, we are sustained by the promise of eternal life and filled with every blessing; help us to live lives that bear witness to you and your incredible goodness to us.*

Twenty-First Sunday in Ordinary Time

At Shechem (nowadays also known by its Arabic name 'Nablus') in the hill country of Ephraim Israel is asked to choose whether to serve God or desert him. They choose to renew their covenant (Joshua 24:1-2, 15-18).

The gospel reading (John 6:60-69) marks another moment of choice: will Our Lord's hearers accept his teaching or 'walk no more with him'? Peter and his companions opt for the former: who else has 'the words of eternal life'?

The union between Christ and his followers is like the intimate union between husband and wife, demanding therefore a firm choice for mutual love and faithfulness (Ephesians 5:21-32).

Once more verses of Psalm 33 make up the responsorial psalm with 'Taste and see that the Lord is good' as its refrain.

Prayerful Ponderings

'I will bless the Lord at all times, his praise always on my lips;
in the Lord my soul shall make its boast. The humble shall
hear and be glad.'

Yet again we hear the psalmist speaking of the spirit of prayerfulness
which characterises his life. Perhaps this time it is an opportunity for
me to measure my own prayer-life against his, to ask: Is praise of
God 'always on my lips'? Do I 'bless' him and praise him in bad
times as well as good? Is he the 'boast' of my life? Or, to put it in a
way which reflects the concerns of today's readings, am I true to the
loving covenant established with me at my baptism and renewed
and deepened every time I 'taste' the gift of the Holy Eucharist?

'The Lord turns his face against the wicked to destroy their
remembrance from the earth. The Lord turns his eyes to the
just and his ears to their appeal.'

The psalmist compares the fate of 'the wicked' with that of 'the
just'. Both groups have made decisive choices (see today's readings),
for while 'the Lord turns his face against' the former, he turns it
towards the latter. The wicked, for all their apparent success and
achievement, are quickly forgotten, and in fact from this point
onwards our attention is centred almost exclusively upon the lot of
the just. They have the Lord's blessing, for 'his eyes' are fastened
upon them - with love and concern; 'his ears' are open to them and
'to their appeal'.

'They call and the Lord hears and rescues them in all their distress. The Lord is close to the broken-hearted; those whose spirit is crushed he will save.'

The just may suffer as do the wicked. They may be numbered - and often are - among 'the broken-hearted' and 'those whose spirit is crushed'; yet they are the ones who know their own weakness and their need of God's help. 'The Lord is close' to them not despite but actually 'in all their distress'. When 'they call' out to him for help, he 'hears and rescues them'; what is certain is that ultimately he 'will save' them.

'Many are the trials of the just man but from them all the Lord will rescue him. He will keep guard over all his bones, not one of his bones shall be broken.'

The psalmist again acknowledges that the just often have to endure many 'trials'; there is no simplistic relationship between good living and trouble-free living. Nonetheless, 'the Lord will rescue' the just, 'he will keep guard over all [their] bones', not one of them will be broken. Our Lord gave a similar assurance: 'even the hairs of your head are all counted. So do not be afraid' (Matthew 10:30-31). Not only did he give that assurance, in his own life he showed how it was to be lived out. He, 'THE just man', faced terrible trials culminating in his death, yet continued to trust his Father. And the Father rescued him from the tomb itself. The crucified and risen Lord is our ultimate source of confidence and trust.

'Evil brings death to the wicked; those who hate the good are doomed. The Lord ransoms the souls of his servants. Those who hide in him shall not be condemned.'

A final glance in the direction of 'the wicked', 'those who hate the good'. It isn't that God destroys them but rather that they destroy themselves: evil is of its nature destructive, death-dealing. How different the fate of 'his servants'. They will be ransomed, not condemned. The word 'ransom' brings to mind Jesus and the bitter price of our ransoming. We can pray this psalm with greater joy and gratitude than did the psalmist; in the Gospels, in a new and wonderful way, we have been able to 'taste and see that the Lord is good'; we have learned from the lips of Jesus himself the unlimited truth in the promise that 'those who hide' in the Lord will not suffer condemnation; as St Paul puts it, 'There is therefore now no condemnation for those who are in Christ Jesus' (Romans 8:1).

LET US PRAY: *We pray, Lord God, that throughout all the twists and turns of life, we may always choose to follow Jesus our Lord and Master.*

Twenty-Second Sunday
in Ordinary Time

A passage from Deuteronomy (4:1-2, 6-8) speaks of the Law as a gift from God, pointing the way to true wisdom, to the fulfilment of the covenant, to a full and happy life.

However, as the gospel shows (Mark 7:1-8, 14-15, 21-23), when the Law becomes an idol and there grows up an obsessional concern with human additions to the Law, then God's real purpose is lost. A change of heart is called for.

The letter of James (1:17-18, 21-22, 27) makes it clear that we who have been made God's children are obliged not simply to listen to his Law but to live by it, especially in our dealings with others.

The responsorial psalm comes from Psalm 14. It is one of two 'entrance' psalms, so called because they list the requirements of those who would worthily enter into the presence of God.

Prayerful Ponderings

'Lord, who shall dwell on your holy mountain? He who walks without fault; he who acts with justice and speaks the truth from his heart.'

To 'dwell on your holy mountain' means to present oneself – even for a short period – before God in the Temple on Mount Zion. The opening question is as relevant today as ever it was: What sort of people are we who come into God's presence? What sort of people should we be? Significantly, the question is addressed to the 'Lord', for only he has the right to stipulate who shall come to worship him; it is helpful for us to remember that we always come as invited guests. The answer, given in his name by a temple priest, begins with a list – by no means exhaustive – of the typical characteristics that a true worshipper should display. Walking 'without fault' may sound too negative; it obviously refers to one who positively keeps God's Law; perhaps the sense is best captured in the expression 'a person of integrity'. Such a one 'acts' with justice, and 'speaks' in a way that mirrors what is in his or her heart. Indeed, the refrain to today's responsorial psalm describes such a person as 'just'. 'The just will live in the presence of the Lord'.

'He who does no wrong to his brother, who casts no slur on his neighbour, who holds the godless in disdain, but honours those who fear the Lord.'

The idea of speaking the truth in the previous verse is continued in this: the just person will not wrong a 'brother' or sister, will not cast a 'slur' on them, either by slander or by scandalmongering. Holding 'the godless in disdain' and honouring 'those who fear the Lord' are not as harsh as they sound. They may amount to nothing more than an unequivocal statement of where the just person stands - for good, against evil.

'He who keeps his pledge, come what may; who take no interest on a loan and accepts no bribes against the innocent. Such a man will stand firm for ever.'
A further description is given of the way just people treat others: they are true to their 'pledge' in all circumstances; they 'take no interest on a loan' in the sense that they do not trade on the misfortunes of others; and they never succumb to 'bribes'. The final statement summarises the whole psalm: those who live according to the teaching of this psalm will not only be admitted to worship; they 'will stand firm for ever', never shaken, enjoying fullness of life. It is important to note that the psalm is not saying that only those who attain such perfection as has been outlined can be admitted to worship: if that were the case, which of us would be found worthy? Rather it is reminding us that sincere worship carries consequences: it anticipates a standard of behaviour which we must at least aspire to.

LET US PRAY: *Lord, we long to honour you not merely with lip service but from the depths of our heart. Help us then to live lives of integrity, to be honest and just and loving in all our dealings with others so that one day we may be admitted to your holy mountain where we may dwell with you and worship you for ever.*

Twenty-Third Sunday in Ordinary Time

The prophet promises that God will come to heal eyes that are blind, ears that are deaf, lips that are dumb, limbs that are lame, and to turn thirsty ground into springs of water (Isaiah 35:4-7).

There is fulfilment of the promise in today's gospel (Mark 7:31-37); but Jesus does not merely make the deaf hear and the mute speak; he opens ears to faith and looses tongues to spread the good news.

A superb illustration is given in the second reading (James 2:1-5) of how genuine faith is incompatible with making invidious distinctions between rich and poor.

Today's responsorial psalm is taken from the hymn of praise, Psalm 145, particularly those verses which speak of the Lord's concern for the poor and weak.

Prayerful Ponderings

'My soul, give praise to the Lord.'
The Psalter ends with a group of psalms – Psalm 145 is the first of them – known as the 'Hallel' collection because each of them begins with 'Halleluiah' – 'praise the Lord'. (There are in fact other Hallel collections in the Psalter but this is the final one.) The psalm is addressed not to others but to the self ('my soul'); the following verses offer reasons for my praise.

'It is the Lord who keeps faith for ever, who is just to those who are oppressed.'
The Lord is deserving of my praise because he 'keeps faith for ever', he is the ever-reliable one; in particular he has a special concern for those 'who are oppressed' in any way, as the man in today's gospel joyfully discovered. And if I praise him for his amazing goodness, I must also strive to imitate him by showing practical compassion for those in need.

'It is he who gives bread to the hungry, the Lord, who sets prisoners free.'
Again, he is the one who 'gives bread to the hungry', but as a rule he does it only with our co-operation. It hurts my conscience that in a world where no one need go hungry about one-third of the human race is starving. The Lord releases 'prisoners', not necessarily

by freeing them from their prison cells but by being with them in their loneliness and enabling them to make something positive of their time 'inside'. Again, it hurts my conscience that Christians are sometimes accused – and as a former prison chaplain I believe not without foundation – of being more punitive and vindictive in their attitude towards wrongdoers than are other groups of people.

'It is the Lord who give sight to the blind, who raises up those who are bowed down, the Lord who loves the just, the Lord, who protects the stranger.'
There is praise for the Lord because of the generosity of his dealings, summed up in a series of brief statements, each of which is substantiated by episodes in the pages of the Gospels. He brings 'sight to the blind' (like Bartimaeus: Mark 10:46-52), 'raises up those who are bowed down' (like the woman bent double; Luke 13:10-13), 'loves the just' (like the poor woman who gave of her poverty': Luke 21:14) but also 'protects the stranger' who has noone to care for him or her (like the leper: Mark 1:40-45).

'The Lord upholds the widow and orphan, but thwarts the path of the wicked.'
In the Old Testament the expression 'the stranger, the widow and the orphan' is regularly used as a kind of shorthand for all those who are defenceless, alone, without power or influence. But though they appear to be 'nobodies', they are dear to 'the Lord', upheld by his special protection, unlike 'the wicked' whose path he 'thwarts'. My conscience is pricked at the thought that I'm often tempted, like the man in the second reading, to give preferential treatment not to the poor and down-at-heel, as the Lord does, but to the well-dressed and the wealthy.

'The Lord will reign for ever, Zion's God, from age to age.'
This final verse assures us that 'the Lord' reigns for ever, which is
another way of saying that his loving attitude towards others will
never change. He is our God, for we are 'Zion', the people of God,
and therefore we must for ever praise him, above all praise him by
living lives of love towards others.

LET US PRAY: *Great King of all the universe, open my mouth to praise
you all my life, open my ears to be attentive to your word, galvanise my legs
and my whole being so that I may become your instrument in service to the
poor and needy.*

Twenty-Fourth Sunday in Ordinary Time

Today's first reading (Isaiah 50:5-9) is known as the third Servant Song: it speaks of a mysterious servant of the Lord who despite dreadful suffering continues to trust in God.

Jesus is indeed the Christ, as Peter confesses (Mark 8:27-35), but Jesus insists he is a Messiah destined to suffer and die. He heads towards Jerusalem in the spirit of the Suffering Servant of Isaiah.

In the gospel Jesus says his disciples must take up the cross and follow him. St James (2:14-18) points out that faith without corresponding deeds is bogus: we are not true disciples if we fail to imitate Jesus in his concern for the hungry, the naked, the sick and the poor.

The responsorial psalm, which comes from Psalm 114, is in the form of a song of thanksgiving from a psalmist who, like the Suffering Servant, faced suffering with trust in God and came through successfully.

Prayerful Ponderings

'I love the Lord for he has heard the cry of my appeal; for he turned his ear to me in the day when I called him.'
The psalm opens with a declaration of love. It would be unsafe to imagine that it is a simply self-centred love, or that the psalmist has come to love God only because he 'turned his ear' to the psalmist's prayer. The love was already there – wasn't it that which gave the psalmist confidence to make 'the cry of... appeal' in the first place? – and now that love is more firmly based than ever, and needs to be openly expressed. When someone very dear to us responds to a request for help, we feel more deeply than ever in his or her debt, and may well express our thanks in terms of love: 'I do love you, you're so kind.'

'They surrounded me, the snares of death, with the anguish of the tomb; they caught me, sorrow and distress. I called on the Lord's name. O Lord my God, deliver me!'
The psalmist rehearses what he's been through; apparently he has endured some severe illness and it seemed that 'the snares of death' were already surrounding him, like some fierce animal ready to pounce; 'the anguish of the tomb' already filled his soul. In such extremity there was no one who could help, save God himself. So it was that 'I called on the Lord's name' and called on him with great confidence, addressed him as 'my God', a God who has a

personal interest in the sufferer. Whether the psalmist had in fact faced a fatal illness or some other affliction, a mental breakdown, say, it should not be difficult for us to apply it to any severe trial we have to endure: in our anguish we too can turn with confidence and call to the Lord.

'How gracious is the Lord, and just; our God has compassion. The Lord protects the simple hearts; I was helpless so he saved me.'
This verse captures the joyful praise of the psalmist, who speaks with enthusiasm - an enthusiasm springing from personal experience - of God's graciousness, of his 'compassion', of the protection he offers to 'simple hearts', those who are humble enough to seek his help. 'I was helpless so he saved me' puts us in mind of St Paul's boast: 'When I am weak, then am I strong.' So long as we rely upon ourselves, we deprive ourselves of God's help, but once we recognise our helplessness, then we are open to the strength that comes from him.

'He has kept my soul from death, my eyes from tears and my feet from stumbling. I will walk in the presence of the Lord in the land of the living.'
The psalmist attempts to explain what the Lord's intervention has meant - a 'soul' kept from impending 'death', 'eyes' freed from 'tears' and 'feet' from 'stumbling'. Little wonder then that he now resolves to 'walk in the presence of the Lord' so long as life shall last. This psalm, which came to be used at the Passover, would have been on Jesus' lips as he went to the Garden of Gethsemane. He did not ask to be saved from tears, from stumbling or even from death (see today's gospel); but he was saved out of sufferings and out of

death. And so, like the psalmist, we can pray this psalm after a recovery from sickness, but, like Jesus, we can also pray it gratefully even in the face of death itself, knowing that we share his resurrection victory.

LET US PRAY: *Gentle and compassionate Lord, sufferings are an inescapable part of life; give us courage never to doubt your love, but to give you thanks that through the resurrection of Jesus we are able to look forward to being raised from suffering and even from death to eternal life.*

Twenty-Fifth Sunday in Ordinary Time

A passage from the book of Wisdom, written in the first century BC, describes how the wicked conspire against the just person (Wisdom 2:12, 17-20) because he or she stands as a reproach to their way of life.

Jesus, the just one par excellence, tells how he will be persecuted by his contemporaries; and he warns his competitive disciples that it is in the person of a little child, not of someone high and mighty, that they will be able to welcome him (Mark 9:30-37).

The second reading (James 3:16-4:3) also speaks of the jealousy and ambition that often fill the human heart, but which stand in complete contrast to 'the wisdom that comes down from above'.

Finally, the responsorial psalm, which is virtually the whole of Psalm 53, reflects the confidence of the just person who despite every difficulty trusts in the Lord.

Prayerful Ponderings

'O God, save me by your name; by your power, uphold my cause. O God, hear my prayer; listen to the words of my mouth.'

This brief psalm is typical of the category to which most psalms in the Psalter belong: it is a plea for help, uttered by an individual – hence, 'me', 'my cause', 'my prayer', 'my mouth' – who invokes the 'name' and the 'power' of God. God's name stands for God himself; here name is used almost synonymously with power, and so the verse becomes a profession that God's very person is powerful. Buoyed up by that belief, the psalmist makes a confident prayer that this mighty God will 'save me', 'uphold my cause', 'hear my prayer' and 'listen to [my] words'.

'For proud men have risen against me, ruthless men seek my life. They have no regard for God.'

The reason for the petition is the plotting of 'proud' enemies who 'have risen against me'. They are 'ruthless', not only because they 'seek my life' but also because 'they have no regard for God'. As the picture emerges of a just person being persecuted by the wicked, it is not difficult to identify with the sentiments expressed in the book of Wisdom (see first reading) nor with those that must have been in the heart of Jesus himself as he faced the persecution he knew awaited him in Jerusalem (see gospel).

'But I have God for my help. The Lord upholds my life.'
Again, in a way that is typical of these individual psalms of petition, there is a statement of confidence ('I have God for my help'). Often, as here, the statement is closely linked with a profession, at least implicit, of trust ('The Lord upholds my life').

'I will sacrifice to you with willing heart and praise your name for it is good.'
A final element in a typical individual psalm of petition is thanksgiving, which usually takes the form of a promise of sacrifice ('I will sacrifice to you') and/or of praise ('I will praise your name'). When, as on this day, the psalm is used as the responsorial psalm of the Mass, it takes on an altogether richer significance. 'With willing heart' we come to thank our Lord and Master who, amid the mockery and scorn of his enemies, 'endured the cross, disregarding its shame' so that he 'has now taken his seat at the right hand of the throne of God' (Hebrews 12:2). We offer the sacrifice which gives perfect praise and thanksgiving to our God and has won a place for us in the kingdom.

LET US PRAY: *In the power of the name Jesus, the name above every other name, we ask you, Father God, to strengthen us when others mock us on your account so that we may remain resolute in our faith.*

Twenty-Sixth Sunday in Ordinary Time

Today's readings sound a note of warning against the small-mindedness which seeks to restrict God's gifts. The book of Numbers (11:25-29) tells how Moses rejoiced that two elders not present for the official 'enrolment' were nonetheless recipients of the Spirit, but reprimanded those who opposed them.

In the gospel (Mark 9:38-43, 45, 47-48) there is reprimand for apostles who try to stop a man from expelling demons on the grounds that he 'is not one of us'. Jesus' attitude is so much more generous: 'anyone who is not against us is for us'.

Psalm 18, which features as today's responsorial psalm, is a powerful song in praise of God's law, whose very purpose is to make us God-like in our attitudes.

As James shows in the second reading (James 5:1-6), those who are attached to riches at the expense of the poor and needy are totally unGod-like.

Prayerful Ponderings

'The precepts of the Lord gladden the heart.'

This sentence, the refrain to today's responsorial psalm, sums up the message of the psalm as a whole. God's 'precepts' have an incomparable value; they 'gladden' the human 'heart' for when rightly understood they are seen to be in our own best interests, they show us how to live God-like lives.

'The law of the Lord is perfect, it revives the soul. The rule of the Lord is to be trusted, it gives wisdom to the simple.'

There are many different ways of describing God's 'law': in this poem alone it is spoken of as his 'precepts', as his 'rule', as 'fear of the Lord', as his 'decrees'. It serves to remind us that law is a much broader concept than any simply legalistic one. In all its manifestations it reveals God's will for us. It might be most helpful to think of it as the voice of God. It is a voice which speaks to us in a multitude of ways: in the Ten Commandments, in the whole of Scripture, in the teaching of the Church, in the events of daily life, and so on. In its Constitution on the Church in the Modern World, Vatican II beautifully describes human conscience as 'people's most secret core, and their sanctuary'; and it goes on: 'There they are alone with God whose voice echoes in their depths' (16). Responding to God's voice, which is always 'to be trusted', brings about a revival of 'soul'; it means a sharing in that profound 'wisdom' that belongs to 'simple' and lowly souls.

'The fear of the Lord is holy, abiding for ever. The decrees of the Lord are truth and all of them just.'

There is a 'fear of the Lord' that is healthy, and 'holy'; it is the kind of fear that arises from love, the kind of fear we all have in relation to those who are dear to us: we dread to think that we might ever do anything that would displease them in any way. It is the kind of fear that we trust will abide 'for ever'. When God makes his will known to us, we know that it is 'truth' and justice.

'So in them your servant finds instruction; great reward is in their keeping. But who can detect all his errors? From hidden faults acquit me.'

This statement follows upon all that has gone before: if we strive to be attentive to God's voice, we shall be rightly instructed, we shall be discoverers of his will. And deep in our hearts we shall know that there is 'great reward' in keeping his instructions; even in this life it brings a deep contentment of mind and heart; it moulds us in the image of Jesus the Lord. There may well be hidden 'errors' and sins in our lives, in the sense that none of us can see ourselves as God sees us, and so with the psalmist we plead that we may be set free from our 'hidden faults', that is to say, faults hidden from us – not necessarily from those with whom we live!

'From presumption restrain your servant and let it not rule me. Then shall I be blameless, clean from grave sin.'

There is a final important request to be made: that our genuine efforts, and even success, in keeping God's law may never lead us into 'presumption', into complacency, into judgement of others, into narrow-mindedness (see today's readings). In the end it is only by God's power and God's forgiveness that I, his 'servant', can ever hope to live a 'blameless', an integrated, life.

LET US PRAY: *May our consciences be always on the alert, Lord God, to hear your voice; and our hearts always ready to respond, so that day by day we may grow in likeness to Jesus Christ your Son.*

Twenty-Seventh Sunday in Ordinary Time

There is no mistaking the main thrust of today's readings; they celebrate the joy of a happy family life, though without ignoring the fact that ideals are not always attained.

The first reading (Genesis 2:18-24) adopts a popular style in picturing God as the author of sex and marriage. Man and woman are of equal dignity and their union is meant to last and bring fulfilment.

In Our Lord's day, just as in our own, the ideal was not always achieved: what is to be done when marriage fails? In response Jesus points to the principle, founded on the will of the creator, that the marriage bond is for ever (Mark 10:2-16).

Psalm 127, which is used in its entirety today, is in praise of a happy family life.

The letter to the Hebrews (2:9-11) speaks of how completely Jesus took on himself our human condition, even to the extent of experiencing death.

Prayerful Ponderings

'O blessed are those who fear the Lord and walk in his ways! By the labour of your hands you shall eat. You will be happy and prosper.'

This little psalm is one of fifteen which were sung by pilgrims as they made their way to Jerusalem. It begins with the words 'O blessed', which might be better translated: 'O the blessings of'. There are blessings from God for those 'who fear the Lord', who live in accordance with his law, allowing it to affect them in every area of life, and so 'walk in his ways'. They will 'labour', like the rest of humankind, but it will be rewarding labour, enabling them to earn food for themselves and their family. In a sentence: they 'will be happy and prosper'.

'Your wife will be like a fruitful vine in the heart of your house; your children like shoots of the olive, around your table.'

They will have the joy of a 'wife' who is 'like a fruitful vine', a symbol of sexual attractiveness as well as of fruitfulness. Their 'children' will cluster round their 'table' like so many olive shoots. The wife is described as being, literally, in 'the innermost parts of the house' - the psalmist, like his contemporaries, believed that the appropriate place for a woman was behind the scenes! - but the translation we have here ('in the heart of your house') is more acceptable to us, for no greater praise could be given to any wife and mother than to acknowledge her as 'the heart' of the 'house' and the family.

'Indeed thus shall be blessed the man who fears the Lord.'
This, says the psalm, is how 'the man who fears the Lord' will be 'blessed'. Alas, life is not always as simple as that (see today's gospel): living a law-abiding life is no absolute guarantee that all will be well domestically. Good men and women often have to struggle with difficult, even broken, marriages. However, it is still true that God-fearers of every generation always recognise that a happy family life is one of the greatest blessings of 'the Lord'. We can go further and say that God wants every marriage to succeed, and even when a marriage fails he is still close to those who suffer as they strive to make sense of their lives.

'May the Lord bless you from Zion in a happy Jerusalem all the days of your life! May you see your children's children. On Israel, peace!'
At this point the psalm becomes a prayer that the blessings of the Lord may stream out 'from Zion', the sacred place where God dwells, bringing happiness 'all the days of your life'. Such happiness includes the joy of living to 'see your children's children'; and, if all this should seem a little too self-centred, there is a final plea that all 'Israel', the whole people of God, will enjoy that rich fulfilment that is summed up in the word *shalom*, 'peace'.

LET US PRAY: *We give you thanks, Lord our God, for the gift of marriage and ask you to bless all married people that in their lives together they may discover a rich symbol of their relationship with you and may make their homes a foretaste of heaven for themselves and their children.*

Twenty-Eighth Sunday
in Ordinary Time

Wisdom is praised above all other goods; in comparison with Wisdom 'riches' are 'as nothing' (Wisdom 7:7-11).

The sad story of the man who refused Jesus' call because he was too wedded to his possessions, serves to underline the value of true wisdom which teaches the paradox that those who lose everything with Christ gain everything (Mark 10:17-30).

The gospel is borne out by the statement of the second reading that Jesus, as the Word of God, cuts more finely than any two-edged sword (Hebrews 4:12-13).

Psalm 89, often described as a 'wisdom' psalm, is a meditation on the brevity of human life and a plea for that wisdom which will enable us to exploit life to the full, despite its shortness, and to appreciate God's unfailing love.

Prayerful Ponderings

'Fill us with your love that we may rejoice.'
This sentence, the refrain to today's responsorial psalm, represents the underlying theme of the whole song. The psalmist begs that the Lord may 'fill' our hearts with his 'love'; it is the assurance of that love that enables us to face life, however short and whatever its ill fortunes; indeed, not merely to face life but to be of good heart and to 'rejoice'.

'Make us know the shortness of our life that we may gain wisdom of heart.'
However, rejoicing in the Lord and his love does not mean blinding ourselves to other aspects of reality, such as the fact that our hold on life is precarious. Indeed, the psalmist positively invites us to 'know', not in some superficial way but in our very bones, that 'life' is short. That realisation can help us to see things in true perspective and so produce in us – and this is what the psalmist prays for – genuine 'wisdom of heart', the ability to discern God's purposes. If this be so for those, like the psalmist, who have not heard the good news of the gospel and so have little or no conception of eternal life, how much more for Christians who know that all life in this world is homeward bound. All things take on their true worth *sub specie aeternitatis*; it is the light of eternity that gives people a wisdom that can lead them to surrender all things in order to follow Christ (see today's gospel).

'Lord, relent! Is your anger for ever? Show pity to your servants.'

The psalmist now seems to take a different tack - but an understandable one, all the same. We may acknowledge that life is short – we may even share the Christian belief in eternal life – but it does not necessarily follow that we want to die! The psalmist seems to have a sense of personal sinfulness and to see the brevity of life as a punishment, arising from God's justifiable 'anger'. In the earlier part of the poem, which does not feature in today's responsorial psalm, God was visualised as 'turning' humankind back into dust, but now, with a play on words - the Hebrew word *shub* (= turn back) is here used in the sense of 'relent' - he is urged to turn back with 'pity to your servants'.

'In the morning, fill us with your love; we shall exult and rejoice all our days. Give us joy to balance our affliction for the years when we knew misfortune.'

The truth is that we need God's help each day if we are to live life wisely. And so with the psalmist we pray that each 'morning', each new day, we may be filled with God's steadfast 'love'; it will enable us to 'exult and rejoice all our days', whatever they may bring. Boldly the psalmist asks that the 'affliction' of years gone by will now be balanced by 'joy'. More boldly still, Paul declares that there will be 'an eternal weight of glory' (2 Corinthians 4:17) to offset all the sorrows and sufferings we have known in this life.

'Show forth your work to your servants; let your glory shine on their children. Let the favour of the Lord be upon us: give success to the work of our hands.'

Finally, a prayer that the kindly 'work' that God does for his 'servants' will continue to be experienced, and that with it they, and their 'children' too, may experience a glimpse of 'your glory'. And the prayer continues with the plea that the Lord's 'favour' will be 'upon us' and all that we do, for without his blessings life loses its purpose and its value.

LET US PRAY: *Teach us, good Lord, never to lose sight of the shortness of life, nor ever to doubt your love towards us; and so may we live wisely and joyfully to the glory of your name.*

Twenty-Ninth Sunday in Ordinary Time

The passage from Isaiah (53:10-11) is part of the fourth Servant Song which describes how through his sufferings the mysterious servant will 'justify many'.

We confidently approach the throne of God's grace, says the letter to the Hebrews (4:14-16) because Jesus, our 'supreme high priest', is already there, having endured all the trials we go through.

Jesus tells his disciples that they are not above their Master, who gave 'his life as a ransom for [the] many', that they too must drink the chalice of trial and suffering if they wish to be seated with him in glory (Mark 10:35-45).

The responsorial psalm, which comes from Psalm 32, is filled with trust in the God whose eyes are upon us and who rescues us from death.

Prayerful Ponderings

'The word of the Lord is faithful and all his works to be trusted.' The psalm begins with a call to praise and to give thanks to the Lord (see verses 1–3), and now the reason for that call becomes clear: God's creative 'word' expresses itself in deed, in 'his works'. It is never empty, always achieves its purpose, and so can be described as utterly 'faithful'. Like 'his works', his 'word' can 'be trusted' in all circumstances.

'The Lord loves justice and right and fills the earth with his love.' The Lord's unlimited righteousness and justice are inevitably reflected in his creation, but still more it is 'his love' that shines out from all that he has made and in all that he does. In Isaiah 6 the prophet has a vision in which he sees the whole earth filled with the glory of the Lord; the psalmist speaks as though he had had a similar vision, but, for him, it is 'with his love' (*hesed*) rather than his glory that the earth is filled. That statement is the key to the whole psalm: it is the Lord's unswerving faithfulness and love that stand as the ultimate explanation of all that is and the ultimate basis for our trust in him.

'The Lord looks on those who revere him, on those who hope in his love, to rescue their souls from death, to keep them alive in famine.'

Against the background of the preceding verses, it is no surprise that the psalmist gives the assurance that 'those who revere [the Lord]', 'those who hope in his love', can always be sure of his attentive care: he 'looks [down]' on them with affection, rescues them from the things that threaten their well-being. Of course, this is no guarantee that we shall never have to face troubles and sorrows (see the Suffering Servant in the first reading), but it is a guarantee that if and when these things do come our way, the Lord will enable us to 'drink the chalice' (see gospel). Indeed, in a way that the psalmist would not understand, we are confident that even when the Lord does not protect us from dying, he 'rescues' us from death all the same.

'Our soul is waiting for the Lord. The Lord is our help and our shield. May your love be upon us, O Lord, as we place all our hope in you.'
Having heard the reasons for trusting in the Lord, we now join the psalmist in declaring that we wait for him, patiently, confident that in the midst of all the trials and difficulties of life he is 'our help and our shield'. And so a final plea – and this forms the response for today's psalm – that, 'as we place all our hope' in the Lord, so his 'love', his faithful goodness, may be 'upon us'.

LET US PRAY: *Lord, you alone are our hope; all our trust is in you. Look upon us, therefore, 'with quick-eyed love' that we may always be sure of your help and support.*

Thirtieth Sunday
In Ordinary Time

Jeremiah (31:7-9) promises the people in exile that there will be another Exodus: they will be restored to their own land, God's love will again be triumphant.

The account of the miracle in the gospel (Mark 10:46-52) reveals another type of restoration, that of sight to a blind man.

In the letter to the Hebrews also (5:1-6), the theme of compassionate restoration appears: Jesus is our compassionate high priest, offering a sacrifice which restores us to our divine sonship and daughterhood.

Psalm 125 is another of the Songs of Ascent; like others in the series it is characterised by brevity (the whole psalm makes up today's responsorial psalm), repetitions and a focusing on Zion.

Prayerful Ponderings

'When the Lord delivered Zion from bondage, it seemed like a dream. Then was our mouth filled with laughter, on our lips there were songs.'

Here is a psalm which breathes something of the joy and relief that first greeted the deliverance of 'Zion from bondage'. We are not told the nature of the bondage. It is tempting to think that it is a reference to the restoration that followed the exile, and that may indeed be the case. However, there are other possibilities, such as release from famine, or siege, or a decline in the city's fortunes. At any rate, it involved such an incredible turn of events that 'it seemed like a dream' and it 'filled' the people with delirious happiness: 'laughter' lighting up their faces and 'songs' of joy 'on (their) lips'.

'The heathens themselves said: "What marvels the Lord worked for them!" What marvels the Lord worked for us! Indeed we were glad.'

Even 'the heathens' were impressed; they found themselves having to admit: 'What marvels the Lord [has] worked for them!' And they were right; we too acknowledged all that he had done on our behalf, and we were overjoyed. The latter two sentences sum up the first part of this psalm and form the refrain for the responsorial psalm; they express the sentiments of the returning exiles (first reading) and of a blind man whose sight is restored (gospel); but they can also voice our own feelings of gratitude as we recall God's ceaseless outpouring of blessings.

'Deliver us, O Lord, from our bondage as streams in dry land. Those who are sowing in tears will sing when they reap.'

At this point the psalm moves in a different direction: it now becomes a petition for God's help, though it is petition made with confidence because it is based on experience of his help in times past; just as he delivered us from bondage then, so may he deliver us from bondage now. May the deliverance bring about a transformation like that which takes place when 'streams' run along the parched watercourses of the 'dry land' of the Negeb. When that happens 'tears' of sadness will turn into songs of joy: the hard graft of 'sowing' will give place to the happy task of reaping.

'They go out, they go out, full of tears, carrying seed for the sowing: they come back, they come back, full of song, carrying their sheaves.'

The second word-picture of the previous verse is now enlarged. Whereas the work of spring rains results in almost immediate change - green shoots quickly appear - the work of farmers is an altogether more protracted affair: 'they go out' to their back-breaking work, it's a tearful task; but in due course 'they come back' and then, the hard times are forgotten because they are 'carrying their sheaves' and they are 'full of song'. The uncertainty surrounding the nature of the original situation which gave birth to this psalm (see above) has a most fortunate result: a song which spoke to its own times, is now able to be applied to almost any difficult situation in which we may find ourselves today. In particular, it might remind us that whenever there are genuine 'tears' of repentance, there is the 'joy' of entering into the marvellous peace that the Lord's forgiveness brings.

LET US PRAY: *Lord, as we reflect on the marvels you have worked for us, may we have absolute confidence that ultimately our tears will be turned into joy, our painful sowing into delightful reaping.*

Thirty-First Sunday
in Ordinary Time

The exhortation to obey all God's commands ends with a reaffirmation of the first and greatest of them all: to love God with all one's heart, soul and strength (Deuternomy 6:2-6).

In his response to the scribe (Mark 12:28-34) Jesus indicates a further dimension to the great commandment: genuine love of God is inseparable from love of neighbour.

The second reading (Hebrews 7:23-28) speaks of Jesus as 'the ideal high priest'; he it is who by his act of sacrifice has proved his boundless love for his Father and for us, his sisters and brothers.

Psalm 17 is one of a small group of thanksgiving psalms. A few verses from it make up today's responsorial psalm; they express our love for him and our praise for all that he has done for us - and all that he is for us.

Prayerful Ponderings

'I love you, Lord, my strength, my rock, my fortress, my saviour.' The first part of this verse, which serves as refrain to the responsorial psalm, sums up what our instinctive reaction to God's goodness should be: an outpouring of love in return, an 'I love you' expressed in deeds as well as in words, and directed to our sisters and brothers as well as to God himself (see the gospel). The psalmist acknowledges not simply that God gives me strength but that he is 'my strength'. The implications of that are brought out in the following words: he is as secure, as dependable, as a 'rock'; as sturdy a defence as a 'fortress'; he is 'my saviour', setting me free from all that threatens my truest interests.

'My God is the rock where I take refuge; my shield, my mighty help, my stronghold. The Lord is worthy of all praise: when I call I am saved from my foes.'
The psalmist returns to the notion of God as 'the rock'; it is the metaphor most commonly used throughout the Psalter to express the stability and reliability of support provided for all who 'take refuge' in him. The list of descriptions of God – the longest list to be found in the Psalter – continues. He is 'my shield', the type of shield large enough to cover the body almost completely; he is 'my mighty help' or, literally, 'the horn of my salvation', a reference to the horns fixed to the altar in Jerusalem which offered safety to

anyone who grasped them after fleeing to the sanctuary for safety; finally, 'my stronghold', the one who, 'when I call' upon him, saves me 'from my foes'. Such a 'Lord' is surely 'worthy of all praise'. It is significant that the psalmist prefaces each description of God with the possessive pronoun 'my', and of course we may do the same: God is related to us not only as a group but also as individuals, so that each of us can call upon him as 'my God'.

'Long life to the Lord, my rock! Praised be the God who saves me.'
Yet again God is addressed as 'my rock'. It may seem rather strange to wish him 'long life'. In fact a better translation would probably read 'The Lord lives!' - as in the Revised Standard Version - where the sense is that 'the Lord' is a living God, unlike the lifeless 'gods' that others worship. To this living God 'who saves' - again in contrast with other deities - praise is supremely due.

'He has given great victories to his king and shown his love for his anointed.'
These words suggest that the psalm was, at least in part, a thanksgiving to God for 'great victories' secured by the 'king'. At the time of the psalm's composition the king in question was David or one of his successors. But the fact that it continued to be sung long after the monarchy had disappeared indicates that the victories gained and the king who, under God, had won them are provisional: they look to the future. It is in Jesus, 'his king', 'his anointed' (= Messiah), that they achieve their fulfilment. It is he who has won the greatest victory of all and through that victory, re-presented at every Eucharist, God has 'shown his love' for his Son but also for all of us who share in his Sonship.

LET US PRAY: *In giving thanks to you, our great God, for all that you have done for us through your Son, Jesus, we pray that we may make a fitting return by striving to fulfil the two great commandments of love.*

Thirty-Second Sunday in Ordinary Time

Widows were among the most vulnerable people in biblical times because they had no bread-winner to support them, and yet (1 Kings 17:10-16) it is a poor widow who sacrifices her last scraps of bread for the prophet Elijah. She does not go unrewarded.

In the gospel passage (Mark 12:38-44), too, it is a widow who wins the praise of Jesus: others may give generously to the temple treasury from their surplus, she gave 'everything she possessed'.

The letter to the Hebrews (9:24-28) tells of a still greater sacrifice, that of our High Priest, who sacrificed himself 'to do away with [our] sin'.

The responsorial psalm is taken from verses in Psalm 145 which praise God for his concern for the poor, including of course the widows.

Prayerful Ponderings

'My soul, give praise to the Lord.'
These words, which make up the refrain for today's responsorial psalm, focus attention on the overall purpose of the psalm. It is to encourage us to join the psalmist in calling upon 'my soul' or, as we might say, our innermost self to 'give praise to the Lord' for the care which he shows, especially for the poor and lowly, such as the widows in today's readings.

'It is the Lord who keeps faith for ever, who is just to those who are oppressed. It is he who gives bread to the hungry, the Lord, who sets prisoners free.'
In a previous verse, not included in the responsorial psalm, the psalmist has reminded us that with the best will in the world human benefactors are never entirely reliable, if for no other reason, because they have no secure hold on life: they can die at any time. But in contrast, the psalmist continues, 'the Lord ... keeps faith for ever'; because he is the ever-living God, he is the most reliable Benefactor of all, as well as the most generous. In particular he has a special concern for the outcasts: 'those who are oppressed', those who go 'hungry', those who suffer imprisonment.

'It is the Lord who gives sight to the blind, who raises up those who are bowed down. It is the Lord who loves the just, the Lord, who protects the stranger.'

The story of the Lord's generosity continues: it is no surprise that he 'loves the just', but what is unexpected is that his love should stretch out to 'the blind', to 'those who are bowed down' by the troubles of life, to those who are 'strangers' and therefore in danger of being ill-treated; and this love stretches out to them because he is moved with compassion for them in their unhappy condition. As we read this psalm we're constantly reminded of Jesus – of his mission statement in the synagogue at Capernaum, telling how he had come to bring good news to the poor, proclaim release to captives and recovery of sight to the blind, and to let the oppressed go free (Luke 4:18); and also of his miracles, for example, restoring sight to a blind man, enabling a women who had been 'bowed down' for eighteen long years to straighten herself up and be free, restoring a dead son to his widowed mother.

'The Lord upholds the widow and orphan but thwarts the path of the wicked. The Lord will reign for ever, Zion's God, from age to age.'

To the list of needy people spoken of in the previous verses there is now added 'the widow and [the] orphan'. Together with strangers, widows and orphans were regarded as the most needy and vulnerable members of society, though as today's readings show it is often these 'little ones' who are most generous to others. 'The Lord will reign for ever,' says the psalmist confidently, but we know that that will only be true if we reflect his kindness and compassion to those who are in need, for he has no hands, no feet, no heart to work for others – except our own, for we are his people, the people of 'Zion'.

LET US PRAY: *You are a Lord who keeps faith for ever, especially with the weak and needy. Lord, may we respond to your desires by our care and concern for the outcasts and the marginalised of today.*

Thirty-Third Sunday in Ordinary Time

The book of Daniel, written about 160BC at a time of persecution and distress, gives one of the few unambiguous references in the Old Testament to resurrection from the dead and eternal life (Daniel 12:1-3).

The coming of Jesus is the beginning of the 'last times', spoken of by the prophets; but it is useless to speculate on the day and the hour of his return in glory (Mark 13:24-32).

The second reading (Hebrews 10:11-14, 18) assures us that Christ has already 'offered the one single sacrifice' that takes away sin and so enables us to look towards the future without undue fear.

Psalm 15, especially the verses which form today's responsorial psalm, speak of trust in God, of delight at his being 'my prize' and of confidence in eternal happiness at his right hand.

Prayerful Ponderings

'Preserve me, God, I take refuge in you.'

Against the background of the end-time, referred to in the readings of today's Mass, this psalm enables us to express our trust in 'God'. We confidently call upon him to 'preserve' us, to keep us safe, when that day comes, whether it be the Last Day or the day of our death (which will be the last day of this world for us!). And at the same time we proclaim that we 'take refuge' in him; he is our only ultimate security.

'O Lord, it is you who are my portion and cup; it is you yourself who are my prize.'

The words of this verse sit with peculiar appropriateness upon our lips. Through the sacrament of baptism, God has entered into a special relationship with us whereby he has become our 'portion and cup'. In the book of Joshua similar vocabulary is used to describe how a particular portion of the Promised Land was divided out to this or that particular tribe; the Lord himself is the special portion that has come to us. He himself is our 'prize', and, like St Paul, our task is to 'press on towards ... the prize of the heavenly call of God in Christ Jesus' (Philippians 3:14).

'I keep the Lord ever in my sight: since he is at my right hand, I shall stand firm.'

Ideally, at any rate, 'the Lord' is 'ever in [our] sight': as our life's history is unfolded, we strive to keep an ever-watchful eye upon him and his plans for us. The thought that he is always 'at [our] right hand' gives us unflagging confidence; even in the face of the end-time which will one day come, we can boldly say: I will not be moved, 'I shall stand firm'.

'And so my heart rejoices, my soul is glad; even my body shall rest in safety. For you will not leave my soul among the dead, nor let your beloved know decay.'

It is such thoughts as those rehearsed in the preceding verses that fill hearts with rejoicing and souls (inmost selves) with gladness. They enable us to look death in the eye, confident that we 'shall rest in safety', our souls will not be left 'among the dead'; we are God's beloved sons and daughters, final decay will not be allowed to touch us. The fact that Jesus was rescued from the tomb is our supreme source of confidence that even death cannot separate us from our God.

'You will show me the path of life, the fullness of joy in your presence, at your right hand happiness for ever.'

Whatever life may bring, there is the deep-down conviction that 'you will show [us]' and, more than that, will lead us in 'the path of life', that there is an absolute fullness of joy' that awaits us when we are brought into 'your presence', and that 'at your right hand' we shall experience a 'happiness' that will know no end.

LET US PRAY: *Keep us safe, O God, in the midst of life's trials and temptations, and keep firm and vital our confidence that we are one day to abide with you and enjoy - heart, soul and body - the happiness of heaven.*

Solemnity of Christ the King

In a mysterious passage in the book of Daniel (7:13-14), the Son of Man, a figure in human form, comes on the clouds towards God, to receive an everlasting and universal kingdom.

The book of Revelation (1:5-8) puts flesh on Daniel's words as it promises that Jesus, having rescued us from our sins by his blood, will be made manifest amid the clouds and all eyes will see him in his royal glory.

In the gospel (John 18:33-37) Jesus affirms that his kingdom is not of this world (see comments below) - but it is a kingdom, nonetheless.

Psalm 92, this Sunday's psalm, is the first of a series of songs running to Psalm 99 which (with the sole exception of Psalm 93) salute God as King. Some scholars have suggested that there was an enthronement festival at which God was invested with kingship. However, the truth surely is that these psalms, like today's feast, far from celebrating his enthronement are simply proclaiming, and celebrating, once again, the good news of God's eternal reign.

Prayerful Ponderings

'The Lord is king, with majesty enrobed; the Lord has robed himself with might, he has girded himself with power.'
The first four words are a proclamation – you can almost hear the herald making the solemn announcement – 'The Lord [God] is king', but he is a king unlike any other (see today's gospel). The psalmist's comments serve to indicate the unique nature of his kingship. Other kings may be marked off from their fellow human beings by wearing splendid royal robes, at least on formal occasions, but here is a 'king' who has no need of such superficial trappings. His 'majesty', 'might' and 'power' are adornment enough, they are the proofs of his royal supremacy over all creation. (As we reflect on this psalm today, the figure of Christ the King will surely be in our minds.)

'The world you made firm, not to be moved; your throne has stood firm from old. From all eternity, O Lord, you are.'
The firmness of 'the world' is due not to its own inherent stability but to the fact that it was brought into being by the Great King and, according to his plan, it is 'not to be moved'. It is a firmness which reflects, or rather is a correlation of, the stability of the royal 'throne' itself: the Lord is visualised as assuming sovereignty by his act of creation, and that sovereignty in its turn is the guarantee of the world's security. Just as his attributes are signs of a unique

kingship (see previous verse) so too is the fact that he, unlike earthly kings, is king 'from all eternity'; there never was a time when he was not king.

'Truly your decrees are to be trusted. Holiness is fitting to your house, O Lord, until the end of time.'
The 'decrees' of the king are surely 'to be trusted'. The word used here for 'decrees' seems to refer not so much to the laws which govern the natural order, such as the law of gravity, but to those which govern the moral order. The implication, therefore, is that the well-being of humanity is as much dependent upon observance of the moral law as the security of the world is dependent upon the functioning of the laws of nature. Such an understanding leads naturally to the conclusion that 'holiness' is the only 'fitting' response to God's kingship; as St Paul says: 'God's temple is holy, and that temple you are' (1 Corinthians 3:17). The psalm ends with a further reminder of the unique character of this king whose 'house' will endure 'to the end of time'- and, as the reading from Revelation shows, eternally beyond.

LET US PRAY: *'Teach me, my God and King,*
In all things thee to see
And what I do in anything
To do it as for thee.'
(George Herbert)

OTHER FEASTS

that may be celebrated on a Sunday

The Ascension of the Lord

This festival has been celebrated with full solemnity since the fourth century as the final, glorious manifestation of our Lord's Easter exaltation, and Sunday by Sunday we profess our belief that 'he ascended into heaven'

On this day, in each year of the three-year cycle, the first reading is always the same; it is the story of the ascension, as recounted by Luke in the Acts of the Apostles (1:1-11). Having instructed the apostles over a period of forty days, Jesus promises them the gift of the Holy Spirit will enable them to be his witnesses 'to the ends of the earth'; then, he is lifted up until hidden from their sight by a cloud. As they gaze into the sky, an angel reminds them that until the day when Jesus returns, they have a job to do.

As though enlarging on the angel's message, the gospel passage (Mark 16:15-20) recalls Our Lord's command to the Eleven: 'Go out to the whole world; proclaim the Good News to all creation'. With that command goes the promise that they will continue his mission by casting out evil spirits and healing the sick, and will be protected from harm.

Psalm 46, from which today's responsorial psalm is drawn, was originally used as part of a solemn procession, perhaps one that brought the Ark of the Covenant, the sign of God's presence, into the Temple. There may even have been some kind of enthronement ceremony in recognition of God's everlasting kingship.

St Paul (Ephesians 4:1-13) implores his hearers (ourselves) 'to lead a life worthy of your vocation' and proceeds to map out the virtues to be cultivated if unity of mind and heart within the Church is to be ensured; it is a unity rooted in one Lord, one faith one baptism. Paul's vision of the Church is of a body in which every member promotes the well being of the whole so that ultimately the Church becomes 'fully mature with the fullness of Christ himself'.

Prayerful Ponderings

'All peoples clap your hands, cry to God with shouts of joy! For the Lord, the Most High, we must fear, great king over all the earth'.

If in days gone by the people of Israel were encouraged to 'clap [their] hands' and 'cry … with shouts of joy' as they saw the ark of the covenant being borne in solemn procession to the Temple, how much more should we be encouraged to celebrate on this great day – even if our celebrations are a little more subdued – when we honour Our Lord's being lifted up from this earth and borne into heaven itself. The scripture readings we've heard today make it clear that everything possible must be done to ensure that one day 'all peoples' will join in our ascension day celebrations: with us they will honour a king who, though like to us in all things, is in fact 'the Lord, the Most High', a king whom 'we must fear', not because he is a tyrant but because he is so awesome and great. Such a one is by right 'great king over all the earth'.

'God goes up with shouts of joy; the Lord goes up with trumpet blast.'

It's hard to listen to these words, which make up the refrain of today's responsorial psalm, without sensing that something special is happening: they take us to the heart of the celebration. There's 'joy' in the air; besides the rhythmic clapping (see previous verse) and the shouts of delight, there is the sound of the 'trumpet', the ram's horn trumpet (*shophar*) whose 'blast' marks important occasions, such as the New Year (Numbers 29:1) or the accession of a king (2 Kings 9:13) or, most significantly in this context, the occasion when David brought the ark to the city to make Jerusalem into God's abode (2 Samuel 6:15). And when the people proclaimed in this psalm: 'God goes up', 'the Lord goes up', was it part of a dramatized renewal (perhaps an annual renewal) of the first time the ark entered the temple? And did they actually see the ark once more mounting towards the doors of the Temple where it would be enthroned? In any event today, through the liturgy, the ascension of the Lord is truly re-presented in our midst so that, with the eyes of faith, we see Our Lord returning to the Father's house, and with joy we can cry out that the Lord does indeed go up.

'Sing praise for God, sing praise, sing praise to our God, sing praise. God is king of all the earth. Sing praise with all your skill.'

Again and again, again and again, the cry goes up: 'Sing praise'. We have all heard a crowd giving vent to its feelings, not necessarily bad ones, by repeating some brief catch phrase over and over again. The very insistence of the cry to praise God in this psalm – 'sing praise for' him, 'sing praise to' him – suggests that it served a similar purpose, and it's easy to visualize the whole assembly chanting these words which sum up the sentiments of all. On this day a similar cry goes out from the Church: we are all invited to raise our voices in praise of the Lord, who has been raised to his heavenly throne as 'king of all the earth'.

'God is king over the nations; God reigns over all the earth'

Though praise of God is important, even vital, yet by itself it is not enough. We cannot, dare not, forget that Jesus' final word to his disciples on the day of his ascension was in the form of their commissioning: their task was to be his witnesses to his message to the ends of the earth. On each subsequent Ascension Day the Church - and we are the Church – is called upon to renew its efforts to make known that 'God is king over the nations', whether they know it or not, that 'God reigns over all the earth', and wants his reign to be acknowledged.. More even than that, he wants all people to hear the good news that he 'has passed beyond our sight, not to abandon us but to be our hope' (Preface of the Mass for the Ascension).

LET US PRAY: *Lord our God, fill us with joy as we celebrate the ascension into heaven of our Lord Jesus Christ. Help us so to live our lives in this world that others will be brought to know and love him as King and God, and finally, where he, the Head, has already gone, may we, his members, most surely follow.*

The Body and Blood of the Lord

In Year 'B' of the three-year cycle, blood is the aspect of the Eucharist which this day's readings focus upon. It's worth noting that St Paul speaks of 'Communion in the blood of Christ' even before he mentions 'communion in the body of Christ' (I Corinthians 10:16).

The first reading (Exodus 24:3-8) is part of a description of the ceremony which sealed God's covenant with his people on Mount Sinai. In fact the ceremony involved two rituals, one a shared meal, the other a blood rite; only the latter is recalled in today's Mass. For Israel, as for people throughout the ancient world, blood was a sign of life, and life belongs to God. When in the ritual on Sinai, blood was sprinkled, first, on the altar, which symbolised God, and then on the people, it was a powerful way of proclaiming that the people now belong to God, share God's life, have become God's blood relatives. This idea is taken up in the responsorial psalm, made up of verses from Psalm 115, where the covenant people express their gratitude for all that the Lord has done for them and their readiness to fulfil their own responsibilities to him.

The gospel (Mark 14: 12-16, 22-26) speaks of a new covenant, so much more wonderful than the one of old. It too is sealed by a sharing in a meal and a blood ritual, but in this case, the second reading (Hebrews 9:11-15) reminds us, the blood is not that of animals but of God's own Son, so that we literally share in his own life, become his blood sisters and brothers.

Prayerful Ponderings

'How can I repay the Lord for his goodness to me?'
On this great feast day, the first thought that comes to mind might well be in the form of a question, the question with which the responsorial psalm begins: 'How can I repay the Lord for his goodness to me?' It's a goodness he has shown in so many ways, but perhaps most touchingly of all by inviting me to share his Body and Blood in the Eucharist. When people love each other, they long to be united as closely as possible, but only our great God could have devised a means of union so intimate as that provided by the Blessed Sacrament. How then can we thank our God?

'The cup of salvation I will raise; I will call on the Lord's name'.
The answer is not long in coming, and it serves as the refrain of the responsorial psalm. We give thanks by raising 'the cup of salvation'. For the psalmist that may have meant a libation cup, poured out as part of a thanksgiving sacrifice, but for us it is the cup of the Eucharist, the Paschal cup which is the new covenant in Christ's blood and the source of our 'salvation'. There is no more eloquent way of 'call[ing] on the Lord's name'.

'O precious in the eyes of the Lord is the death of his faithful. Your servant, Lord, your servant am I; you have loosened my bond.'
It's difficult to know how the first of these two sentences was

originally meant to be understood. But in view of the fact that the Lord has 'loosened [the] bond' of his 'servant' (see second sentence) and so allowed him to live, perhaps what is meant is that 'his faithful' are too 'precious' for God to allow them to die. In any event on this day we ought indeed to give thanks that through the precious blood of Christ we have been saved from eternal death, we have been loosed from the bonds of our sins, we have been washed clean.

'A thanksgiving sacrifice I make: I will call on the Lord's name. My vows I will fulfil before all his people'.
Again there is promise of 'a thanksgiving sacrifice' or, in our case, the thanksgiving sacrifice, the Mass which we are now celebrating. Along with gratitude goes the resolve to fulfil '[our] vows before all his people'. Conscious of our being incorporated into the people of God by the shedding of Christ's blood, we resolve to 'fulfil' our covenant obligations to him by practical action so that we may be a source of encouragement to others. As has been powerfully suggested, to receive Christ in Communion with great fervour and then deliberately hurt our sister or brother is like leaning forward to kiss a friend without realising that you 'are trampling on his feet with nailed boots!' 'Whatever you do to the least of my brethren …'

LET US PRAY: *We give thanks, O good Jesus, for the mighty gift of your most precious Blood in the Eucharist; through it we have become your own kinsmen and women; may it so fire us in mind and heart that we will be a source of inspiration to others, to the praise and glory your Name, together with that of Father and Holy Spirit.*

The Presentation of the Lord (February 2)

Though for many centuries this feast was called the feast of the Purification of the Blessed Virgin Mary, its earlier title, one it had from its origin in the fourth century, was the Presentation of the Lord. The restoration of that title is a reminder that, like all Marian feasts, this one points to the indestructible link between Mary and her Son: it is through her that he is presented.

When Mary presents the Child, the prophecy of Malachi (3:1-4) is fulfilled, for he speaks of a day when 'the Lord will enter his Temple' – though he could never have believed that the Lord would arrive in the form of a babe-in-arms!

The second reading, taken from the letter to the Hebrews (2:14-18), underlines the reality of Our Lord's humanity. Like any other first-born Jewish child, he had to be 'redeemed' forty days after his birth; like any one of us, he had to grow to maturity and, like any one of us, he was tried and tempted.

The gospel story (Luke 2:22-40) is something more than a bare account of the way in which Mary and Joseph complied with the Law. It serves as a formal announcement of Jesus' arrival in the Temple, his presentation to his people and, still more, his presentation to Jews and Gentiles alike as 'the salvation' of all humankind.

The second half of Psalm 23 is this Sunday's responsorial psalm. The earlier part speaks of the Lord as Maker and King of all creation and provides instruction on those who may worthily enter his presence; this part is applied to the arrival of the Lord himself in the Temple.

Prayerful Ponderings

'O gates, lift up your heads; grow higher, ancient doors. Let him enter, the king of glory!'

It seems likely that this psalm, especially this part of it, was composed as an accompaniment for a procession in which the ark of the covenant, the symbol of the Lord's presence, would be solemnly brought to the Temple, and there a festival celebrated in honour of his Kingship. In poetic language, the huge 'gates' which stand at the threshold of the Temple are commanded to 'lift up [their] heads' and the 'ancient doors' to 'grow higher', as though the entrance needs to be enlarged if it is to cope with the towering figure of the invisible Lord who is about to enter his palace, seated upon the ark as upon a throne. Nothing must be allowed to hinder the entry of 'the king of glory'.

'Who is the king of glory? The Lord, the mighty, the valiant, the Lord, the valiant in war.'

We can perhaps imagine the priests calling out, from inside the Temple, 'Who is [this] king of glory?', and back coming the response: 'The Lord, the mighty, the valiant'. We may find it difficult to feel sympathy for such a warlike God! However, the fact is that especially in earlier times the God of Israel was regarded as a mighty warrior: after all, he was more powerful than the pagan gods, and they, according to their adherents, had brought creation into being after the defeat of fierce enemies, and so, it was sometimes argued, Yahweh must have done the same; again, the people of Israel were confident that he had accompanied them, riding on the ark (which served as his chariot), when they went out to battle, so that they confidently styled him 'valiant in war'. Under the influence of the prophets these warlike titles came to take on a more general significance: they were ways of pointing to his greatness, his power, his holiness.

'O gates, lift high your heads; grow higher, ancient doors. Let him enter the king of glory.'

Once more the cry is raised that the gateway be enlarged to allow entry to 'the king of glory'. This time we might listen to it against the backcloth of today's feast. In the arms of Mary and Joseph, Jesus is coming to his Temple, coming to present himself as our Redeemer, 'the salvation … for all the nations', the one who restores us to God's friendship, the one who stands not only as 'the glory of … Israel' but also as 'a light … to the Gentiles' (hence, today's candle ceremony). And we are being invited to open the doors of our hearts to him, to rid ourselves of whatever might stand in the way of his coming, to enable him to become for us 'the king of glory'.

'Who is he, the king of glory? He, the Lord of armies, he is the king of glory.'

If the repeated query about the identity of 'the king of glory' again results in a warlike response, 'the Lord of armies', we have only to look at the tiny child in the arms of Mary and Joseph to realise that many faulty views about God stand in need of revision as a result of the incarnation. Ever since this child was born in the stable at Bethlehem, forty days ago, we have been gently reminded that our God is 'the king of glory' not only because he is all-powerful but also because he is so humble as to 'empty himself' and become 'completely like his brothers [and sisters]' (second reading). It is precisely through this self-emptying even to death on a cross that he has conquered in the only battle that matters, that against sin and Satan, and so set us free. Significantly, though the response to today's psalm is based on this verse, and its earlier counterpart, the answer it gives to 'Who is the king of glory?' makes no mention of military prowess; it states quite simply: 'It is the Lord.'

LET US PRAY: *Jesus, Son of God and Son of Mary, you are Lord. Come into our hearts, defeat all our spiritual enemies and be now and for ever our King of glory.*

Birth of John the Baptist
(June 24)

Four passages in Isaiah speak of a mysterious 'servant' of the Lord who suffers much but is the bearer of God's good news. Christian tradition has applied them to Jesus, but today's liturgy applies the second of them to John the Baptist, called as God's servant 'from my mother's womb', commissioned to bring Israel back to God and destined to be 'the light of the nations' (Isaiah 49:1-6).

The second reading (Acts 13:22-26), from Paul's sermon to the Jews at Antioch, speaks of John as the one who 'heralded' the coming of the Saviour and 'proclaimed … repentance' which is the precondition of conversion to the Lord.

The subjects of today's gospel (Luke 1:57-66, 80) are John's birth, the wonder surrounding his naming and the 'awe' which filled those present, leading them to wonder: 'What will this child turn out to be?'

Psalm 138, 'The Hound of Heaven' psalm, as it has been called, is a most appropriate psalm for today's feast, with its reference to God's knowledge and power which affect even those as yet unborn.

Prayerful Ponderings

'O Lord, you search me and you know me, you know my resting and my rising, you discern my purpose from afar. You mark when I walk or lie down, all my ways lie open to you.' This awesome and attractive psalm - unfortunately, only a few of its verses appear in the responsorial psalm - acclaims the unique character of God's knowledge, power and presence. John the Baptist, whose birth we celebrate today, must often have reflected on the wonderful relationship that existed between himself and God. Perhaps in the last dark days of his life, when he was being held captive in a subterranean dungeon by King Herod, he would have prayed this psalm, confident that God's discerning eye, which had always been upon him, was upon him still; that God's knowledge extended to even the most mundane of his everyday activities, such as 'my resting' and 'my rising', 'when I walk' and 'when I lie down'; that God's ability to read the human heart enabled him to 'discern [my] purpose from afar' - it was clear to God even before it was properly formed in the herald's own mind. However, this psalm is not just for great saints or for those who play an obviously crucial role in the Lord's plans; it is for everyone. Each of us can give thanks that our God is so close, that his loving knowledge of us is so all–embracing, that his understanding of us and our plans is so complete, that 'all [our] ways lie open' before him.

'For it was you who created my being, knit me together in my mother's womb.'

The words of the psalmist would have been particularly apt on the lips of John the Baptist, for John was born in answer to his parents' fervent prayers, even though both were old and Elizabeth 'was barren'. Not only John's birth and the events surrounding his circumcision, but even the fact of his conception must have caused the people to marvel and to wonder aloud: 'What will this child [so obviously due to God's intervention] turn out to be?' However, again we are invited to recognise that 'it was [the Lord] who created my being', it was he who 'knit me together in my mother's womb'. I am unique: not an accident but part of God's great design.

'I thank you for the wonder of my being, for the wonders of all your creation.'

Even the psalmist could appreciate the incredible craftsmanship that goes into the fashioning of a human being. And so the psalmist felt the need to thank God 'for the wonder of my being'; and that act of gratitude led on to a prayer of thanks for 'the wonders of all your creation'. Today we know so much more about the wonder of a human being – scientists have even mapped the human genome ('the language in which God created life', as President Clinton described it) – and yet perhaps there is still nothing so calculated to fill us with wonder as the sight of a newborn baby. People tend to express their astonishment as they take hold, for example, of the child's tiny fingers, and say with a sense of awe: 'Isn't he perfect! Isn't she wonderful!' Each of us is one of 'the wonders of [his] creation'; but through Jesus, whose coming was heralded by John, a still greater wonder has been worked in us: we have been re-created as sons and daughters of God.

'Already you knew my soul, my body held no secret from you when I was being fashioned in secret and moulded in the depths of the earth.'

This verse summarises what has gone before: it tells how we are known through and through, 'soul' and 'body', by the God who made us. Even when were being 'moulded in the depths of the earth', a metaphor for the hiddeness of the womb, we 'held no secret from him'. It is indeed a cause for wonder and gratitude that he who made the stars and the seas and the earth, was also involved in our prenatal development, fashioning us down to the tiniest detail so that we are, as the RSV translation puts is, 'intricately woven'. Again we need to remind ourselves on this day that God's creative work is involved not only in the fashioning of the great saints like John the Baptist but also of every single human being who is ever conceived.

LET US PRAY: *God our Father, on this day as we rejoice in the birth of John the Baptist, herald of our Saviour, we give thanks that through the saving work of Jesus Christ we, who are wondrously made, have become sharers in his divine Sonship.*

Saints Peter and Paul
(June 29)

Today's first reading (Acts 12:1-11) records how, when Peter was imprisoned, 'the Church prayed to God for him unremittingly' and how he was miraculously released.

Paul is able to make the proud boast: 'I have fought the good fight to the end... I have kept the faith'. But he acknowledges that it was the Lord who 'rescued [him] from the lion's mouth' and prays that glory may be given to him for ever (2 Timothy 4:6-8, 17-18).

The gospel (Matthew 16:13-19) is the account of Peter's recognition of Jesus as 'the Christ' and Jesus' designation of Peter as the rock on which 'I will build my Church'.

Today's psalm is taken from the first part of a song of thanksgiving (Psalm 33) which praises God, in particular for the psalmist's own experience of deliverance.

Prayerful Ponderings

'I will bless the Lord at all times, his praise always on my lips; in the Lord my soul shall make its boast. The humble shall hear and be glad.'

The psalmist boldly proclaims his resolve to 'bless the Lord at all times', to have 'his praise always on my lips', to ensure that only 'in the Lord my soul shall make its boast'. Moreover, it is his belief that 'the humble', those who are attuned to the Lord's ways, will rejoice with him and 'be glad' when they 'hear' what the Lord has done for him. Such sentiments would surely be dear to the heart of St Paul for he was a truly grateful man. In the first of his letters which has come down to us, he urges his friends in Thessalonica to give thanks to the Lord 'in all circumstances' (1 Thessalonians 5:18). The implication is that that is what he did himself; indeed, the notion of thanksgiving occurs so many times in his subsequent correspondence that it might well be described as one of his theme songs.

'Glorify the Lord with me. Together let us praise his name. I sought the Lord and he answered me; from all my terrors he set me free.'

Both Peter and Paul could look back on situations where they had been set free 'from all [their] terrors' by the intervention of the Lord. Peter was 'sprung' from his prison cell (first reading) despite the elaborate precautions taken against his escape, and Paul recalls how he was 'rescued from the lion's mouth' (though we have no means of knowing what – or who – the lion may have been). So each might have urged the other to 'glorify the Lord with me. Together let us praise his name.' However, on this feast day we are all being invited to join them in glorifying, praising and thanking the Lord for all that he has done through these two great apostles. Once they had discovered, or, better, been discovered by, Christ and recognised him as Lord, they sought him and his will all the rest of their days. Many times they had to face 'terrors' – in the end they had to face the threat of death itself for his sake and that of the gospel – and still they remained confident that 'he [would] set [them] free'.

'Look towards him and be radiant; let your faces not be abashed. This poor man called; the Lord heard him and rescued him from all his distress.'
No one can 'look towards [the Lord]' with faith and trust without becoming 'radiant', without catching a certain likeness to him; it is what Paul seems to be referring to when he says that 'all of us, with unveiled face, seeing the glory of the Lord … are being transformed into the same image from one degree of glory to another' (2 Corinthians 3:18). The apostles would have us know that despite our weakness we need not 'be abashed'; like many a 'poor man [who has] called [on the Lord]', we can be sure that the Lord will hear and will rescue us from 'all [our] distress'

'The angel of the Lord is encamped around those who revere him, to rescue them. Taste and see that the Lord is good. He

is happy who seeks refuge in him.'

Often in the Hebrew Scriptures the expression 'the angel of the Lord' is used of God himself, particularly when he intervenes in human affairs. His presence is like a protective army 'encamped around those who revere him'; he is ready 'to rescue them', whatever their plight. The psalmist's advice is straightforward: 'Taste and see that the Lord is good'; it is as though he were saying: I've given my testimony, now it's up to you to sample the Lord for yourself; then you'll discover that you are safe in his hands. That discovery was certainly made by the two saints we honour today: they are foundations on which the Church rests. Finally, it's worth noting that the advice to 'taste and see that the Lord is good' is applied in the New Testament to Christians who have newly received the sacrament of baptism (1 Peter 2:3), while among the early Fathers of the Church it is also used in reference to the Holy Eucharist.

LET US PRAY: *We pray, Lord our God, that the Church throughout the world may be inspired by the noble apostles Peter and Paul and that, like them, all Christians may taste and experience your unbounded goodness and all-powerful protection.*

The Transfiguration
of the Lord (August 6)

Written when the Jews were reeling under Syrian persecution, the first reading, from the book of Daniel (7:9-10, 13-14), offers encouragement by reminding them, on the one hand, of God in the guise of 'one of great age' ablaze with glory, and, on the other, of God's representative, 'one like a son of man' on whom 'sovereignty, glory and kingship' are conferred and who is worshipped by all the nations. It is that representative who is at the centre of today's feast.

Peter, to whom the second reading (2 Peter1:16-19) is attributed, recalls that what Christians believe are not 'cleverly invented myths' but events of which he, and others, were witnesses. And so, he claims, 'we were with him on the holy mountain' (of transfiguration).

The gospel for this feast (Mark 9:2-10) is always an account of the transfiguration, but, depending upon which year it is within the three-yearly cycle, the passage is taken either from the Gospel of Matthew or that of Mark or that of Luke.

Psalm 96 is one of the 'enthronement psalms', praising God for his universal reign, but also emphasising the fact that he has saved his people.

Prayerful Ponderings

'The Lord is king, let earth rejoice, let all the coastlands be glad. Cloud and darkness are his raiment; his throne, justice and right.'

Much of the imagery in this psalm seems to have been borrowed from the religions of surrounding nations which commonly depicted their 'god' achieving kingship by defeating lesser 'gods' in battle. The psalm begins with a simple but powerful statement - 'the Lord is king' – which will be elaborated in the rest of the song, though in fact only a few verses appear in today's responsorial psalm. To begin with, his kingship is an invitation to the whole 'earth' to 'rejoice' and 'all the coastlands' to 'be glad'. Mysterious 'cloud and darkness' both conceal him and serve as signs of his presence, just as they had been on Mount Sinai (and of course on the mount of transfiguration when Jesus was overshadowed by a bright cloud [see gospel]); they are even looked upon as 'his raiment', his royal robes, while the 'throne' on which he is seated has as its bases 'justice and right'. A royal throne has always been a symbol of kingship, and the Lord's throne could not be more firmly based, for it rests on the twin qualities of justice and right. Justice embraces all those divine actions and decisions which lead to righteousness, to a way of life that is rich and fulfilling.

'The mountains melt like wax before the Lord of all the earth. The skies proclaim his justice; all peoples see his glory.'

Next, the very 'mountains', despite their apparently immovable solidity, are compared to a piece of 'wax' melting away in the overwhelming presence of 'the [mighty] Lord of all the earth'. Meanwhile 'the skies' take up the proclamation of 'his justice': he is a judge who can be depended upon always to acts with fairness and impartiality. And finally there is the promise that 'all people' will 'see his glory'. On the mount of transfiguration the apostles saw their Master so utterly open to the Father that the Father's glory shone through his person and his very garments, while the voice of the Father proclaimed him as his beloved Son. In the liturgy of today's feast we too are granted a vision of Our Lord in glory, one truly like us – 'one like a son of man' as Daniel describes him (first reading) – but at the same time one on whom has been conferred 'sovereignty, glory and kingship'.

'For you indeed are the Lord, most high above all the earth, exalted far above all spirits.'

The refrain of today's psalm is made up of a phrase from this verse of the psalm – 'most high above all the earth' – prefaced by the exclamation 'the Lord is king'. To hail Jesus as Lord is already to hail him as king, is already to acknowledge that he is 'exalted far above' not only all earth and all people but also 'above all spirits'. On this day we are filled with wonder for we see how the Jesus who walked the streets of Palestine has been revealed as glorious image of the Father and as supreme Lord of all creation. He stands for us 'as a lamp for lighting a way through the dark until the dawn [of our resurrection] comes and the morning star rises' [second reading].

LET US PRAY: *We bow down in wonder before you, Lord Jesus, truly the only Son of the Father but also our brother, like to us in all things but sin. As you have shared our common lot of suffering and even of death, so may we one day share in full measure in your heavenly glory.*

The Assumption of the Blessed Virgin Mary (August 15)

The first reading (Revelation 11:19; 12:1-6, 10) comes from a type of literature (apocalyptic) which aimed to give reassurance in time of persecution. 'The woman' it speaks of refers in the first place to the Church: she will survive the Roman offensive that has been mounted against her. But it is also applied to Mary who is mother of the Messiah, mother of the Church and first and most perfect Christian disciple.

Through Christ, the second Adam, has come the hope of resurrection from the dead: he is the first to rise in glory; today's feast teaches us that Mary was the second to share his triumph to the full and is a pledge for us of the resurrection that awaits us beyond death (1 Corinthians 15:20-26).

The gospel for today (Luke 1:39-56) tells the delightful story of the Visitation; it is a story which revolves around the woman who is to bring us our Messiah. Through him will come salvation and the promise of resurrection from the dead. Today we rejoice in the belief that the promise has already been fulfilled – in the Assumption of Mary, body and soul, into the glory of heaven.

Psalm 44, which provides the two verses which make up today's responsorial psalm, was originally a wedding song for a Davidic king but later came to be recognised as Messianic, as achieving its fulfilment in the Davidic king, Jesus Christ; the 'queen' who is shown standing beside him is applied in today's feast to Mary taken up into the heavenly palace of her Son.

Prayerful Ponderings

'The daughters of kings are among your loved ones. On your right stands the queen in gold of Ophir.'

A royal wedding was always an important event and this psalm reflects the magnificence

of such an occasion. Extravagant praise is lavished on the king: 'your ladies of honour' (the translation which the RSV prefers to 'your loved ones') are members of royal families, they are in fact 'the daughters of kings'. But 'on [his] right' in the place of honour – and this is the climax of the passage – 'stands the queen' herself. She is dressed in beautiful robes interwoven with glistening 'gold of Ophir', the most costly gold that could be found. All eyes are on the bride: 'on your right stands the queen, in garments of gold' is the refrain of today's Psalm. We too are meant to fix our eyes upon her, seeing in her the completed model, so to say, of what we all shall be one day, provided only that we are faithful to the Lord. The reference to her vesture of gold might remind us of the many blessings with which God has clothed her to prepare her to be a worthy mother of his Son. However, it is because she responded so wholeheartedly with those graces that she is the symbol of the Church. Moreover, she knows how indebted she is: for ever she will acknowledge (see the Magnificat in today's gospel) 'the Almighty has done great things for me. Holy is his name.'

'Listen, O daughter, give ear to my words: forget your own people and your father's house.'

The king begs his new queen ('daughter' he calls her) to 'give ear to my words', in the double sense of listening carefully to them and acting upon them; in the gospel Mary is portrayed precisely as someone who 'pondered' in her heart all that happened to her, all that was said to her, and at the same time was always ready to respond as the humble handmaid of the Lord. According to this verse, the queen is also called upon to 'forget [her] own people and [her] father's house'. In its original context this rather extreme advice perhaps meant little more than that she must give up her own home and family and enter the king's abode, become part of his family and be totally devoted to him. (It has been suggested that she was a foreign princess and so would literally have had to leave her home and family behind.) Mary too, in becoming mother of the Saviour, had to set out on a new way of life: everything must have been so different for her, perhaps she had to abandon her plans to marry Joseph, certainly she had to be prepared to follow her Son wherever it might take her – even to the summit of Calvary.

'So will the king desire your beauty: he is your lord, pay homage to him.'

'The king' of the psalm may well have been overwhelmed by the physical 'beauty' of his young wife, but it was above all the spiritual beauty of Mary that was so pleasing to the Lord. The queen of the psalm was also reminded that her husband was her 'lord' and that therefore she must 'pay homage to him' - in the days of the psalmist a wife's submission to her husband was taken for granted – but Mary had no need to be reminded of her duties to the Lord;

her whole life was shot through with praise, she desired only to 'magnify the Lord' in all that she did. As the first and perfect Christian she gladly paid him homage.

'They are escorted amid gladness and joy; they pass within the palace of the king.'
The mysterious 'they' of this verse are the queen's bridesmaids. They have known her perhaps from childhood and it is a moment of immense 'gladness and joy' when the solemn moment arrives for the bridal pair and their attendants to solemnly enter 'the palace of the king'. A new life has begun. On this day we celebrate Mary's solemn entry into the palace of the King of kings; but she does not go alone. She is the first of all those who will share her triumph, who, like her, will be taken up body and soul into the glory of heaven.

LET US PRAY: *We beg you, Mary our Mother, to pray for us that, following your example, we may serve the Lord faithfully all our days and at the last enjoy eternal gladness and joy in the palace of Jesus, our Lord and King.*

The Triumph
of the Cross (September 14)

Today's first reading (Numbers 21:4-9) takes us back to Israel's days in the desert. There, because of their rebellion against God, 'fiery serpents' were let loose upon them. Many died. Moses was instructed to erect a bronze serpent on a pole; whoever looked upon it would live.

The gospel (John 3:13-17) draws a striking parallel between the raising up of the serpent in the desert and the lifting up of Jesus on the cross 'so that everyone who believes in him may... have eternal life'.

The second reading (Philippians 2:6-11) is the beautiful hymn from St Paul's letter to the Philippians which records how Jesus, putting aside his glory, humbled himself to the point of death – even death on a cross. By his obedience our rebellions are healed.

The verses which make up today's responsorial psalm are taken from the lengthy Psalm 77 (no less than 70-odd verses long!), one of three great historical psalms which tell the story of God's dealings with his people, especially at the Exodus, during their desert journeyings and on their arrival in the Promised Land.

Prayerful Ponderings

'Never forget the deeds of the Lord.'
A nation forgetful of its own past has been likened to a person suffering from loss of memory. The people of Israel were never in danger of such amnesia because biblical faith is a 'remembering' faith, a faith rooted in history (Guttiérez), a faith which will 'never' allow the people to 'forget the deeds of the Lord'. Though these words are not an exact excerpt from the psalm, they do in fact serve as a perfect summary of it, for time and again throughout the song the importance of remembering is underlined.

'Give heed, my people, to my teaching; turn your ear to the words of my mouth. I will open my mouth in a parable and reveal hidden lessons of the past.'
The opening words of the psalm itself are usually described as 'wisdom instruction'. The 'wise men' or sages in the ancient Near East were renowned for their discernment and teaching ability. They would expect the 'people' to 'give heed… to my teaching', would call upon them to 'turn [their] ear to the words of my mouth' and would promise to speak to them 'in a parable' (or wise saying) and in particular to 'reveal [to them] hidden lessons of the past'. On this day we are invited to be wise enough to listen carefully to the history of our ancestors in faith, for we too have much to learn from it.

'When he slew them then they would seek him, return and seek him in earnest. They would remember that God was their rock, God the Most High their redeemer.'

After the introductory verse, we are led at once to a later section of the psalm which is concerned with the desert wanderings of the people of Israel. Despite all that God had done in rescuing them from slavery in Egypt, they had chosen to murmur against him (first reading), to rebel against him. Then, when he took action against them ('he slew them' is the way the psalmist describes it), 'they would seek him' again, they would 'return and seek him in earnest'. They 'would remember'- the very thing that we are all asked to do today – remember that he is 'their rock', their abiding support, that he is 'God the Most High', that he is 'their redeemer'.

'But the words they spoke were mere flattery; they lied to him with their lips. For their hearts were not truly with him; they were not faithful to his covenant.'

However, their display of repentance, apparently so earnest, was completely deceptive, for 'the words they spoke were mere flattery'. The situation is not unlike that addressed by the prophet Hosea when he told the people, in God's name: 'Your love is like a morning cloud, like the dew that goes away early' (6:4). All that they had said 'with their lips' were so many lies because there was no real repentance, 'their hearts were not truly with him' and that was shown by the way they lived their lives: quite simply, 'they were not faithful to his covenant'. However, on this feast day especially, we dare not forget that we too, despite all our promises and good intentions, continue to fail the Lord in so many ways. As St James reminds us, we still have to learn how to be 'doers of the word and not merely hearers who deceive themselves' (James 1:22).

'Yet he who is full of compassion forgave their sin and spared them. So often he held back his anger when he might have stirred up his rage.'

Thankfully, our God does not treat us as we deserve, for he 'is full of compassion'; just as he 'forgave their sin' and 'spared' his people, so he continues to spare us and forgive us. The psalmist remarks – it sounds almost in unbelief – that 'so often he held back his anger' when what might have been expected was that he would 'have stirred up his rage'. Still more do we have reason to marvel at the long-suffering compassion of our God; over and over again we have to confess our failures and sins – that's the way we begin almost every Mass – and yet we have confidence to believe that he will have mercy and spare us. That lonely figure, hoisted up on the cross of Calvary, is the reason for our hope. If he is prepared to lower himself to this level (see second reading) in order to save us, then we can indeed look up to him in faith and be confident that we shall be healed, no matter how terrible our unfaithfulness.

LET US PRAY: *Lord, may we heed the wise words of the psalmist; may we never forget your mighty deeds and never lose sight of your compassion and your readiness to save; may we recognise the cross of Calvary as the symbol not of tragedy but of glorious triumph.*

All Saints
(November 1)

The first reading (Revelation 7:2-4, 9-14) speaks of the countless host of men and women from every time and place who now see the face of God.

John (1 John 3:1-3) gives us the incredible news that already we are 'God's children' but that we are destined to 'be [still more] like him because we shall see him as he really is'.

In the Beatitudes (Matthew 5:1-12), Jesus speaks of the happiness, the blessedness, of those who are poor, who are gentle, etc. By earthly standards such people may seem to be losers but in fact they are the children of God, destined for 'the kingdom of heaven'.

Psalm 23 is a hymn in honour of the Kingship of the Lord; the verses used for the responsorial psalm are, appropriately for today's feast, in the form of an entrance liturgy, announcing the kind of people who will be allowed into the presence of God.

Prayerful Ponderings

'The Lord's is the earth and its fullness, the world and all its peoples.
It is he who set it on the seas; on the waters he made it firm.'
This opening verse sets the scene for all that follows; we are introduced
to the Lord, to whom belongs the whole of nature, 'the earth and its
fullness', and the whole of humanity, 'the world and all its peoples'. All
belongs to him because he is the great creator. In the psalmist's day the
world was pictured as being surrounded on all sides by a watery waste,
and God himself as conquering the fierce waters, so that he is able to 'set
(the world) on the seas', to fix it on stout pillars so that it will remain
'firm' and secure amidst 'the (heaving, chaotic) waters' of the deep. This
is the God whom the pilgrims are now about to approach.

'Who shall climb the mountain of the Lord? Who shall stand
in his holy place?'
In the light of the poet's description of the mighty creative work
of God, an obvious question arises: Who would ever be worthy to
'stand in his holy place', to enter into the presence of a God such
as this? Of course the psalmist is thinking only in terms of the
Temple in Jerusalem: before pilgrims ascend 'the mountain' on
which the Temple is built, they wonder who will be able to 'climb
the mountain of the Lord' with good conscience. However, on this
feast day, the question is a more extraordinary one: Who dare think
of entry into God's temple in heaven, entry into the very presence
of God himself?

'The man with clean hands and pure heart, who desires not worthless things. He shall receive blessings from the Lord and reward from the God who saves him.'

The psalmist tries to answer the first question raised by the previous verse, as to who might worthily make his or her way into the Temple. But the answer, provided in all probability by one of the temple personnel, may also be accommodated to the second question, which is concerned with those worthy of entrance into heaven itself. It is those who have 'clean hands and pure hearts' because they do no wrong to others and above all because they have set their heart on the Lord rather than on any 'worthless things'. They are the people spoken of in the first reading: who have been faithful to God through every trial, who 'have washed their robes white ... in the blood of the Lamb'. They are the beatitude people spoken of in the gospel: those who have known their need of God, those who are gentle, those who hunger and thirst for what is right, those who are merciful, those who are peacemakers, those single-minded people who are described by Jesus as 'the pure of heart' and the children of God. Even on earth they bore the likeness of the Lord because of the way they lived their lives and today we celebrate the fact that they are still more wonderfully 'like him' because now they 'see him as he really is' (second reading). The promise has indeed been fulfilled: they have received 'blessings from the Lord' and a 'reward' beyond their wildest dreams. But they will always remember that their eternal reward is due not to themselves but rather to 'the God who saves them'.

'Such are the men who seek him, seek the face of the God of Jacob.'

This verse is also the refrain for today's responsorial psalm. In its original setting it was simply a confirmation that those approaching the Temple were worthy to enter. But today we might use it in the form of a prayer: we are the people 'who seek [you]', we are the people who 'seek [your] face'. The psalm may suggest that those worthy of God's presence are completely perfect, and maybe the readings seem to confirm that same impression. However, among the saints whom we honour today are people whom we have known and loved; many of them are 'ordinary' people, with their weaknesses and defects and sinfulness. They have striven hard but ultimately they are in heaven because of the mercy of God. And the same will be true of ourselves. Despite all our inadequacies – and worse – our hearts are set on God; we do long to see his face and we do trust that he will one day enable us to join that countless throng gathered before his throne.

LET US PRAY: *Great and mighty God, we praise you on this day for all the wonders of your creation but still more for the wonders of spiritual re-creation which you have worked in your saints. We too seek your face; may there come a time when we shall be numbered among those who are honoured on the feast of All Saints.*

The Dedication of the Lateran Basilica (November 9)

Today's feast commemorates the dedication of the Mother Church of Christendom: St John Lateran is the Pope's own cathedral church. The first reading (Ezekiel 47:1-2, 8-9, 12), with its account of a stream of water flowing from the Temple and bringing life wherever it flows, is meant to remind us of the blessings that God bestows upon people everywhere through his Church.

Paul (1 Corinthians 3:9-11, 16-17) describes the Church as a living temple; it is a sacred temple, indwelt by the Holy Spirit and with Jesus Christ as its sole foundation.

In response to those who attack him for his cleansing of the Temple in Jerusalem, Jesus speaks of himself as a sanctuary which, three days after its destruction, he will raise up (John 2:13-22).

Psalm 45 is the first of a group of psalms which hymn the glory of Jerusalem, the Lord's own city. It is because his Temple is founded there that it will stand firm against every assault. Verses from this 'song of Sion' feature in today's Mass: Jesus dwells for ever in his Church.

Prayerful Ponderings

'God is for us a refuge and strength, a helper close at hand, in time of distress: so we shall not fear though the earth should rock, though the mountains fall into the depths of the sea.'
A psalm could hardly begin with a more powerful confession of trust in God. He is saluted as 'a refuge and strength', one who defends us and empowers us in our difficulties, and as one always ready to help us for he is 'a helper close at hand, in time of distress'. In response to such statements of confidence, 'we', the people gathered in worship, declare that 'we shall not fear', not even if those apparently most stable elements, the earth and the mountains, should come to grief. We shall not fear 'though the earth [itself] should rock' and the burly mountains totter and 'fall into the depths of the sea'. St John Lateran is the Pope's own church, and, as an inscription at its east end explains, it is 'Mother and Head of all Churches … throughout the world'. And so on this feast day we are meant to give thanks for the world-wide unity of the Church, a unity which centres around the Holy Father. It was after proclaiming Peter as 'the rock on which I will build my Church' that Jesus promised that, despite enemies from without and scandals from within, his Church would stand firm for ever, and that not even 'the gates of hell' would prevail against it (Matthew 16:18).

'The waters of a river give joy to God's city, the holy place

---

where the Most High dwells. God is within, it cannot be shaken; God will help it at the dawning of the day.'

The mysterious reference to 'the waters of a river' perhaps reflects an ancient belief that the home of the gods is surrounded by a stream which serves as a life-giving source. There is a similar allusion in the description of the river flowing out of the garden of Eden in Genesis 2:10-12, as well as in the account of the life-giving stream in today's first reading. Jerusalem is 'God's city' and 'the holy place where the Most High dwells'; it is his presence that ensures its security against all its enemies; 'at the dawning of the day', when enemies often decide to mount an attack, he will be there to help and protect it. On this feast day we remember with gratitude that the survival of the Church throughout the ages – 'it cannot be shaken' to destruction - is ultimately due to the fact that it stands in the world as the city of God; it is he who dwells in its midst, it is he who ensures that while it is always in need of reform it is also a source of health and holiness for the whole human race.

'The Lord of hosts is with us: the God of Jacob is our stronghold. Come consider the works of the Lord, the redoubtable deeds he has done on the earth.'

The cry 'the Lord of hosts is with us' is a confident declaration that God with his heavenly army of angels is there to defend us. It is not anything we can do that gives us our security, but the fact that he 'is our stronghold'. We have only to consider 'the works of the Lord', says the psalmist, only to reflect on 'the redoubtable deeds he has done on the earth' and, it seems to be implied, we shall have no reason to fear. No doubt the psalmist is thinking of all that God has done for his people throughout their history, beginning with the Exodus from Egypt. But today when we profess our trust in the God who dwells within his Church, we recall 'the redoubtable deeds' that Jesus has accomplished from his birth in the stable of Bethlehem, to his public ministry, to his death and glorious resurrection, to his sending of the Holy Spirit so that the Church might spring to life as his Mystical Body. We know that he will be with us 'always, even to the end of the age' (Matthew 28:20).

LET US PRAY: *On this day, we give thanks that the Risen Lord is the new Temple in which God is worshipped in spirit and in truth, that we have been built up as living stones in that Temple and that bound together in unity under Peter's successor we are confident that the Lord of hosts will be with us throughout the ages.*

The Immaculate Conception of the Blessed Virgin Mary (December 8)

From the first reading of this Mass (Genesis 3:9-15, 20) it becomes clear that today's feast links Mary intimately with her Son; it is her role in salvation history that is stressed. The promise, following upon the 'fall' of our first parents, that there would be a woman whose child is destined to crush the head of the 'serpent' already hints at the work accomplished by the Mother and her Child, Mary and Jesus.

The redemptive work of Christ is beautifully outlined in the second reading (Ephesians 1:3-6, 11-12); the richest beneficiary of that work is Mary, whom the Father 'chose in Christ' from all eternity that she might be 'holy and spotless' and so a worthy mother for his Son.

The gospel account of the Annunciation (Luke 1:26-38) shows Mary being greeted by the angel as 'full of grace', a fullness which she has known from the first instant of her existence.

Psalm 97 is an enthronement psalm, praising the Lord as King. The verses chosen for today's great feast rejoice in the saving work of God and, by implication, in the part that Mary played in that work as mother of the Saviour.

Prayerful Ponderings

'Sing a new song to the Lord for he has worked wonders. His right hand and his holy arm have brought salvation.'

The first sentence, which is the beginning of Psalm 97 and also the refrain of today's responsorial psalm, is a call to 'sing a new song to the Lord'. The song is new not because it is newly composed but because it is an invitation to consider anew the saving work of the Lord, and on this day especially it is a call to praise God for the unique place he has allotted in his plans to the young maiden, Mary of Nazareth. It is a call addressed to all the redeemed, who have benefited so magnificently from the 'wonders' that 'he has worked' through Jesus (see second reading), wonders which are greater even than those worked at the Exodus. Like a warrior, whose hands and arms overcome the foe, Jesus is pictured as overcoming our deadliest foes, sin and death, by 'his right hand and his holy arm'. However, we cannot forget that his hands were nailed to a wooden beam, his arms stretched on a cross in order to achieve our 'salvation'.

'The Lord has made known his salvation; has shown his justice to the nations. He has remembered his truth and love for the house of Israel.'

The first, as well as the supreme, beneficiary of the Lord's saving work is Mary. In her we see what 'salvation' means: it is not simply forgiveness of sin or even preservation from sin (as the title of Immaculate Conception might suggest) but rather something gloriously joyful and positive. Mary is 'highly favoured'; from the first moment of her existence she is so intimately united with God that there is no room for sin in her life, so completely his that she is the embodiment of all we mean by 'salvation' (see the gospel). And so, in her, God 'has shown his justice [his plan to draw all men and women into his friendship] to [all] the nations'; in her he has shown forth his steadfast 'love' for his people, 'the house of Israel': he has been true to all his promises of old.

'All the ends of the earth have seen the salvation of our God.'
The story of the garden of Eden tells of human rebellion against God: abusing the wonderful gift of freedom, human creatures make wrong choices and so separate themselves from God and from one another (see first reading). And yet from the beginning God had already planned to come to our rescue so that we could become 'his adopted sons [and daughters]'. Through Jesus, whose very name means 'salvation', the divine plan is revealed to 'the ends of the earth', and, at the heart of that plan, God has shown his immense respect for human freedom: the coming of the Saviour was made dependent upon the free consent of Mary (see the gospel).

'Shout to the Lord all the earth, ring our your joy'.
The responsorial psalm ends in much the same way as it began, with a summons to praise the Lord, though this time we are invited to 'shout to the Lord' and to 'ring out [our] joy', and the summons goes out to 'all the earth'. Today is indeed a celebration, a celebration of God's merciful goodness, his matchless love for his

creatures, but also a celebration of a woman, one of us, who in view of the motherhood that was to be hers was conceived immaculate (God's favour was always with her) and who when the time came was ready to give her wholehearted consent. And so it was that the Word was made flesh and dwelt among us. Alleluia!

LET US PRAY: *Heavenly Father, you chose Mary from all women to be our advocate with you and our pattern of holiness. Following her example, may we always be ready to say a wholehearted Yes to your designs so that, like Mary, we may bring Christ to others and so continue your saving work in the world.*

APPENDIX

Psalms	Sundays
1:1-4,6	6th Ordinary (C)
4:2,4,7,9	3rd Easter (B)
8:4-9	Trinity Sunday (C)
14:1-5	22nd Ordinary (B)
	16th Ordinary (C)
15:1-2,5,7-11	3rd Easter (A)
	13th Ordinary (C)
15:1,5,8-11	33rd Ordinary (B)
16:1,5-6,8,15	32nd Ordinary (C)
17:2-4,47,51	30th Ordinary (A)
	31st Ordinary (B)
18:8-11	3rd Lent (B)
18:8-10,15	3rd Ordinary (C)
18:8-10,12-14	26th Ordinary (B)
21:8-9,17-20,23-24	Passion Sunday (A,B,C)
21:26-28,30-32	5th Easter (B)
22	4th Lent (A)
	4th Easter (A)
	28th Ordinary (A)
	16th Ordinary (B)
22:1-3,5-6	Christ the King (A)
23:1-6	4th Advent (A)
	All Saints
23:7-10	The Presentation of the Lord
24:4-5,8-9,10,14	1st Advent (C)
24:4-9	26th Ordinary (A)
	1st Lent (B)
	3rd Ordinary (B)
26:1,4,13-14	3rd Ordinary (A)
26:1,4,7-8	7th Easter (A)
26:1,7-9,13-14	2nd Lent (C)
28:1-4,9-10	Baptism of the Lord (A)
29:2,4-6,11-13	13th Ordinary (B)
	3rd Easter (C)
	10th Ordinary (C)
30:2-4,17,25	9th Ordinary (A)

31:1-2:5,7, 11	6th Ordinary (B)
	11th Ordinary (C)
32:1-2,4-5,18-19	5th Easter (A)
32:1,12,18-20	19th Ordinary (C)
32:2-3,7,17-19	30th Ordinary (C)
32:4-5,18-20,22	2nd Lent (A)
	29th Ordinary (B)
32:4-6,9,18-20,22	Most Holy Trinity (B)
33:2-7,9	4th Lent (C)
33:2-9	19th Ordinary (B)
	SS Peter and Paul, Apostles
33:2-3,10-15,9	20th Ordinary (B)
33:2-3,16-23	21st Ordinary (B)
39:2:4,7-10	2nd Ordinary (A,B)
39:2-4,14,18	20th Ordinary (C)
39:7-11	The Annunciation of the Lord
40:2-5,13-14	7th Ordinary (B)
44:10-12,16	The Assumption
45:2-3,5-6,8-9	Dedication of Lateran Basilica
46:2-3,6-9	The Ascension of the Lord (ABC)
49:1-8:12-15	10th Ordinary (A)
50:3-4,12-15	5th Lent (B)
50:3-4,12-13,17,19 + Luke 15:18	24th Ordinary (C)
50:3-6,12-14,17	1st Lent (A)
53:3-6,8	25th Ordinary (B)
61:2-3:6-9	8th Ordinary (A)
62:2-8	32nd Ordinary (A)
62:2-6,8-9	22nd Ordinary (A)
	12th Ordinary (C)
64:10-14	15th Ordinary (A)
65:1-7,16,20	6th Easter (A)
	14th Ordinary (C)
66:2-3,5,6,8	Mary, Mother of God (A,B,C)
	20th Ordinary (A)
66:2-3,4-8	6th Easter (C)
67:4-7,10-11	22nd Ordinary (C)
68:8-10,14,17,33-35	12th Ordinary (A)
68:14,17,30-31,33-34,36-37	15th Ordinary (C)

70:1-6,15,17	4th Ordinary (C)
	Birth of John the Baptist
71:1-2,7-8,12-12,17	2nd Advent (A)
71:1-2,7-8,10-13	Epiphany (A, B, C)
71:1-2,7,34-38	Triumph of the Cross
77:3-4,23-25,54	18th Ordinary (B)
79:2-3,15-16,18-19	1st Advent (B)
	4th Advent (C)
79:9,12-16,19-20	27th Ordinary (A)
80:2-8,10-11	9th Ordinary (B)
83:2-3,5-6,9-10	Holy Family (C)
84:9-12	2nd Advent (B)
84:9-14	19th Ordinary (A)
	15th Ordinary (B)
85:5-6,9-10,15-16	16th Ordinary (A)
88:2-3:16-19	13th Ordinary (A)
88:2-5,27,29	4th Advent (B)
	St Joseph
89:1,3-6,12-14	18th Ordinary (C)
	23rd Ordinary (C)
89:12-17,	28th Ordinary (B)
90:1-2,10-15	1st Lent (C)
91:2-3,13-16	11th Ordinary (B)
	8th Ordinary (C)
92:1-2,5	Christ the King (B)
94:1-2:6-9	3rd Lent (A)
	23rd Ordinary (A)
	4th Ordinary (B)
95:1-3,11-13	Christmas Midnight (A,B,C)
95:1,3-5,7-10	29th Ordinary (A)
	2nd Ordinary (C)
95:1-7	Dedication of the Lateran Basilica
96:1-2,6-7,9	7th Easter (C)
96:1-2,5-6,9	The Transfiguration
96:1-2,6-9	27th Ordinary (C)
96:1,6,11-12	Christmas Dawn (A,B,C)
97:1-6	Christmas Day (A,B,C)
97:1-4	6th Easter (B)
	28th Ordinary (C)

	The Immaculate Conception
97:5-9	33rd Ordinary (C)
99:1-3,5	11th Ordinary (A)
	4th Easter (C)
102:1-2,11-12,19-20	7th Easter (B)
102:1-4,8,10,12-13	7th Ordinary (A)
	8th Ordinary (B)
	7th Ordinary (C)
102:1-4,6-8,11	3rd Lent (C)
102:1-4,9-12	24th Ordinary (A)
103:1-4:24-25,27-30	Baptism of the Lord (C)
103:1,24,29-31,34	Pentecost (A,B,C)
104:1-6,8-9	Holy Family (B)
106:23-26,28-31	12th Ordinary (B)
109:1-4	The Body & Blood of Christ (C)
111:4-9	5th Ordinary (A)
112:1-2,4-8	25th Ordinary (C)
114:1-6,8-9	24th Ordinary (B)
115:10,15-19	The Body & Blood of Christ (B)
115:12-13,15-18	2nd Lent (B)
116:1-2 + Mark 16:15	9th Ordinary (C)
	21st Ordinary (C)
117:1-2,16-17,22-23	Easter Sunday (A,B,C)
117:2-4,13-15,22-24	2nd Easter (A)
117:2-4,15-18,22-24	2nd Easter (B)
117:2-4,22-27	2nd Easter (C)
117:1,8-9,21-23,26,28-29	4th Easter (B)
118:1-2,4-5,17-18,33-34	6th Ordinary (A)
118:57,72,76,77,127-130	17th Ordinary (A)
120	28th Ordinary (C)
121:1-2,4-9	1st Advent (A)
121:1-5	34th Ordinary (C)
122	14th Ordinary (B)
125	30th Ordinary (B)
	2nd Advent (C)
	5th Lent (C)
127:1-5	Holy Family (A)
	33rd Ordinary (A)
	27th Ordinary (B)

129	5th Lent (A)
	10th Ordinary (B)
130	31st Ordinary (A)
136:1-6	4th Lent (B)
137:1-5,7-8	5th Ordinary (C)
137:1-3,6,8	21st Ordinary (A)
137:1-3,6-8	17th Ordinary (C)
138:1-3,13-15	Birth of John the Baptist
144:1-2,8-11,13-14	14th Ordinary (A)
	31st Ordinary (C)
144:2-3,8-9,17-18	25th Ordinary (A)
144:8-9,15-18	18th Ordinary (A)
144:8-13	5th Easter (C)
144:10-11,15-18	17th Ordinary (B)
145:1:7-10	23rd Ordinary (B)
145:2,6-10	26th Ordinary (C)
145:2,7-10	32nd Ordinary (B)
145:6-10	3rd Advent (A)
145:7-10	4th Ordinary (A)
146:1-6	5th Ordinary (B)
147:12-15,19-20	2nd after Christmas (A,B,C)
	The Body & Blood of Christ (A)

Canticles
Isaiah 12:2-6	Baptism of the Lord (B)
	3rd Advent (C)
Daniel 3:32,52-56	Trinity (A)
Luke 1:46-50,53-54	3rd Advent (B)